Life Is A Local Story:
A Collection of Talks Concerning
Local History, Historic Sites,
And History Museums

Edited by
CLEMENT M. SILVESTRO

**THE AMERICAN ASSOCIATION FOR STATE AND
LOCAL HISTORY**

Preface

The papers published in this *Bulletin,* with one exception, were presented at the American Association for State and Local History's annual meeting in Raleigh, North Carolina, October 2-5, 1963, and at the Association-sponsored session of the Western History Association convention in Salt Lake City on October 18. Because the subjects discussed are important to all those who are interested in the state and local history movement, the Association has brought them together in this form.

Not all of the essays are related to each other. Jonathan Daniels, nationally renowned journalist-historian, presented his lucid and witty talk to a receptive audience of historians and archivists at the Association's annual dinner meeting at the Hotel Sir Walter on October 2. His insights concerning the importance of local history, and his affection and gratitude toward those who have worked to preserve the records of local history, will long be remembered by those present.

Unlike Daniel's address, the remaining papers in this *Bulletin* are somewhat more technical, appealing more perhaps to persons associated with history museums and historic sites.

Two sets of papers concern museum interpretation. The first is a series of three papers on "What's New and Effective in Museum Interpretation?". Chairman Frederick Rath's introduction to these provocative papers makes further remarks about them superfluous. The second set includes papers by Merrill J. Mattes, James T. Forrest, and John W. Jenkins at the Western History Association meeting at Salt Lake City. Mattes evaluates the work of the National Park Service in the development of history museums in the West, giving an overview of what the Park Service has done and is now doing, and how it has tried to cope with some of the difficult problems of museum interpretation in the region. Forrest analyzes museum interpretation in western state and local historical societies, emphasizing differences in point of view between exhibit designers and museum curators. Speaking from his long experience in various museums in the West, John W. Jenkins makes some effective comments on both papers.

Closely related to the subject of museum interpretation is the rapid development of historic sites in the United States. Clifford L. Lord of Columbia University has made an independent study of the cost of maintaining these sites and the importance of their location for economic solvency. His paper, not presented at either of the meetings mentioned, is included because of its importance to historic sites administrators and local historians who are using historic sites as combination museum-headquarters.

The cost of maintaining historic sites is directly related to the responsibility for their preservation. The role that all levels of government should play in the preservation of historic sites is the subject of the last set of papers, presented at the Association's annual meeting by Edward M. Riley, Clement M. Silvestro, Margaret B. Tinkcom, and W. Howard Adams.

CLEMENT M. SILVESTRO

Contents

Local History: Story of Mankind

Jonathan Daniels

I am honored and a little intimidated in your presence tonight. It is a pleasure to confront in person so many whom I have bedeviled so long with inquiries at a distance. Still as one of those maybe too many American newspapermen who have had the temerity—or the audacity—to invade the field of the professional historian, I am awkward in your presence. It is one thing to see Chris Crittenden in slacks across the street from my house cutting his own grass. It is another to confront him surrounded by the array of his colleagues who preside over the records and the story of all the parts and pieces of our past.

I miss my friend and schoolmate David Mearns, chief of the manuscript division of the Library of Congress. Were he here, I could reassure myself with the recollection of the times when he was a book boy in that great library and I was a privileged adolescent ranging its stacks. Still I am heartened to see Jim Patton, of the Southern Historical Collection, who has carried off my own papers and whom my wife regards as the most welcome of trash men.

I am torn confronting those who collect our papers and our past. My father kept papers to the despair of janitors in his cluttered office and often to the distress of my mother at home. As she grew old her blue eyes lost much of their vision. But her blindness was not quickly apparent. Generally she knew where father's papers were better than he did. And to protect the appearance of the house which she loved, she found it necessary to add more and more cases and cupboards. One day she called a carpenter to add more. The next day she asked him why he, a different carpenter, was on the job.

"Why, I'm the same man, Mrs. Daniels."

She stared at him doubtfully.

"I can prove it," he told her. "Yesterday when I was at work you said, 'In my next incarnation I will not marry a man who saves a scrap of paper.'"

Fortunately for my wife things have been made simpler. And fortunately for me I've been able to follow archivists and local historians all my life—maybe even prenatally. Before I was born Dr. J. G. deRoulhac Hamilton was rooting in my grandfather's basement for Reconstruction papers. But I was off writing a book about the South when I came on his trail at a decaying plantation in East Feliciana Parish in Louisiana. He had been welcomed there by a charming old lady whose grandmother had been tutored by Audubon. Later he was not regarded with so much welcome by Deep South archivists who came too late to the loot. To them he was J. G. Ransack Hamilton. I suspect you all belong to that tribe.

Presuming that we've got all our own valuable papers locked up, we are happy to have you in North Carolina. The welcome to achivists is hearty even though your distinguished predecessor, Peter Force, was the first scholar to make the still locally astounding suggestion that the Mecklenburg Declaration of Independence was not all our patriots purported it to be. We are happy to have state and local historians here even if there may be some among you who might question the fact, monumented in bronze and marble, on our Capitol Square, that Andrew Jackson was born in North Carolina.

North Carolina is not quite so bound in states' rights doctrines in either politics or history as some other Southern states. Still I am glad that your joint convention puts American archives and local history together. That helps me make a point which might otherwise seem silly. You remember the ridicule which came to General Winfield Scott Hancock as Democratic nominee in 1880. Somebody asked him about the tariff. And said the General, the tariff is a "local question." The guffaws helped elect Garfield. Still I dare the laughter to pronounce the conviction that there is no history except local history. Call concern for it parochialism if you will, it is the only path to the understanding of the world.

Certainly the national or the world historian better know the locales from which his history comes. There is something wonderful about the large stroke and the sweeping theme. Certainly the fashionable history of Arnold Toynbee marks an erudition which seems to encompass the province of all learning. And when such a great one stooped in swift passage to include even a reference to North Carolina in his philosophy of the surges and declines of peoples and places, our bosoms swelled with pride.

You may remember that he wrote: "The former exaltation of Virginia and South Carolina is the veritable cause of their abasement now. They have failed to rise again from their prostration in the Civil War because they have never succeeded in forgetting the height from which that fearful catastrophe once hurled them, whereas North Carolina, who had lost so much less because she had so little to lose, has found it relatively easy to recover from a slighter shock."

The idea has some validity in local history. If we didn't have the big houses to burn, we had the most boys to die. Still, before Mr. Toynbee wrote, a North Carolina historian had described this state as a "militant mediocrity" moving forward because it had less to forget. We know that this state was called the vale of humility between two mountains of conceit before Mr. Toynbee developed the phrase into a parable. Our only regret is that no historian or archivist has ever discovered who invented the phrase. I would be happy to claim it for myself and probably would if there were no vigilant archivists around. The best I have been able to do was to set violent Virginians at my heels once by calling that state the cradle and the grave of democracy. I got off with less furore in South Carolina. I married a South Carolinian. She took me to meet her relatives there. And when we came home I told her that there were only two kinds of South Carolinians: one kind had never worn shoes and the other kind made you feel that you had never worn shoes.

There are other interpretations of this local history. I once irreverently reported that Virginia as the mother of Presidents had not even been pregnant lately. And perhaps impiously I quoted James Louis Petigru as saying in 1861 that South Carolina was not big enough to be a republic. It was too big to be a lunatic asylum.

Mr. Toynbee may be right about us still. It is good to be able to take down his big book as a sort of solace when we are looking at sad statistics. Still I remember that in an early version of his Virginia-North Carolina-South Carolina item of local proof of a world thesis he mentioned Woodrow Wilson in a reference to the biological blossoming of North Carolina. In later versions some state or local historian set him straight. Mr. Wilson as you know was born in Virginia and spent more of his formative years in South Carolina. In his revised version the men Mr. Toynbee picked to prove his point were indeed North Carolinians, but they had to go elsewhere to make their living and prove their powers.

We need our Toynbees. And it may be only evidence that a copyboy can look at a cosmopolite for such an uninvited intruder into history as myself to say that the best history grows up from the details, not down from the generalizations. Still it pleases me to remember in the recent mass invasion of newspapermen into the field of the archivist and historian, that Peter Force was a newspaperman before he began the preparation of his American Archives. And after him came the long roll of newspapermen in our time, Carl Sandburg, Douglas Freeman, Bruce Catton, Lloyd Lewis, Allan Nevins, to name only a few.

They had much to learn from the archivists and the historians. But as a private in the army of invasion I dare suggest that professional historians and archivists might learn from the invaders something in terms of a news sense for the past. Both the historical pros and the journalistic historians, who should perhaps be called the cons, face similar problems and dangers. The quick acceptance of the news handout by the reporter may be no more dangerous than ready dependence upon the engraved document by the historian. Slick public relations in the preparation of both began before our times. Also there may be alternate but equal faults in the feature story and the Ph.D. thesis.

I would not suggest that the historian take his definition of what is history from the definition of news credited to the New York *Sun* editor about man, bite and dog. Certainly state and local historians should not be caught in the news concept attributed to the editors of the rough and rowdy *Denver Post* that a dogfight in Denver is more important than a war anywhere else in the world. Despite local pride in local history the historian must, of course, beware of the faults of sensationalism in the local press. This difficult matter of evaluation recalls the story of the time when an assistant brought to Col. J. B. McCullagh, of the St. Louis *Globe-*

Democrat, some huge wooden type for a head on the story of a tornado in St. Louis in 1896.

"Wonderful!" said the Colonel. "A great head! But really, I was saving that type for the Second Coming of Christ."

One big wind in St. Louis is, of course, not one which necessarily shakes Christendom. Still I am happy to have had some sound archivists and historians, too, lead me to the understanding that details in the distance from great capitals have shaped American destiny and the American story.

The lack of understanding of that is often a fault of contemporary newspapermen. I saw that in surprise when I undertook to write a biography of Harry Truman. Regularly some of the best American reporters accompanied him on visits home to Kansas City. I doubted when I went there hunting that I could find anything my colleagues of the press had not already uncovered. Perhaps with too little modesty, I say that I surprised myself and surprised them. They had taken the handouts, attended the press conferences. But —and sometimes I was happily with them—they had spent more time between spot stories in the bars than in the morgue of the *Kansas City Star*. They read the daily papers but not the old broken-backed city directories giving year by year the various occupations of a young man who often in business as well as in politics was involved in risky enterprises.

I think I see something similar in the case of both newspapermen and historians in the story of Franklin Roosevelt. It seems still the fashion to swing the great drama of his life around the attack of polio. The alteration then in the young, handsome, strutting F.D.R. seems, as often written about, almost like what happened to St. Paul on the road to Damascus. When I undertook to look at his pre-Presidential story at Campobello, at Hyde Park, in the clubs and offices of Washington, in fashionable houses and in political finagling, the faltering gait to greatness did not seem so simple to me. Actually, I am sure the ordeal of Franklin Roosevelt, the great alteration in Roosevelt, was a matter of many acts and events, of personal problems which were personal history and in the truest sense local history, overlooked and disregarded even when much of it took place on the national capital stage.

That has been true of many of our heroes—and villains. When I tried to draw from his place on many local scenes the portrait of a man as the very image of the Carpetbagger, I found the story of

Reconstruction was a mass of local history. It was, of course, not limited to the noisy national capital. It certainly was not limited to the lamenting Southern states. The story of this dashing but forgotten young protégé of Abraham Lincoln, one Milton Littlefield, ran in roguery all across the American scene in and after our best loved war. The national story was a puzzle of local pieces.

An archivist in Illinois found for me a handbill which illuminated Littlefield's story in terms of community draft-dodging in upstate New York. It pointed at bounty graft there, too, on the basis of almost mythological Negro substitutes who never left the South Carolina sea islands where they only hoped to get 40 acres and a mule. Through small public libraries in New York towns I found my Carpetbagger's own archives in the possession of his granddaughter, no inheritor of loot, but a clerk in a Grant store in Philadelphia, a lady with a Lithuanian husband, a broken-backed cat, and a pile of papers.

All the local pieces finally fitted into one national story. I found it different when I turned to purely local history. Certainly it is difficult to think of anything more local than a road rambling only from Nashville in Tennessee to Natchez in Mississippi. But the world traversed it. Spaniards, French, British, then Americans fought for a continent upon it. About it was the scene of the Mississippi Bubble. It was the path to conquest of the continent. Also it was the locale where the coincident development of the steam loom in Manchester, England, and the invention of the cotton gin on the coast of Georgia created the Cotton Kingdom and circumstances which led to the American Civil War.

I was honored when your Association of State and Local History gave me an award for my book *The Devil's Backbone,* the story of the Natchez Trace which was local history about all that and more. But frankly the award left me in doubt as to whether I or you or anybody else knows what is state and local history—or world history either for that matter. You have my thanks and I share with you our puzzle.

Fortunately we don't have to solve it. And fortunately everywhere now more men and women are bringing energy and intelligence to the collecting and the preservation of our history and our heritage. Newspapermen like myself have turned eagerly to appropriate by the double handfuls the magnificent research appearing in historical journals. They only seem dull on their often dun covers. And the popular interest in history everywhere grows—sometimes too fast, it seems to me. It will be a splendid day when every county and town has its history. But frankly I note a tendency to make local histories almost too readable and more dramatic than earlier detailed and inclusive tomes. Suddenly chambers of commerce, tourist bureaus, oil companies, souvenir salesmen, motel operators, are rushing in faster even than newspapermen have done to sieze a share of history for their own purposes.

Recently looking at the North Carolina scene, I wrote that the old three R's of reading, writing and 'rithmetic have been almost supplanted by the preoccupation with the new two R's. They seem to me to be Research and Recreation. Fortunately not all research is devoted to space ships or to centers serving as a basis for attracting industry. Here in North Carolina concern for history has in terms of our Department of Archives and History grown in my own lifetime from a cubbyhole to the present construction of a sort of archivistic cathedral.

History certainly is not neglected in Recreation. All roads lead to the shrines, the restorations. All roads are marked, too, so that he who rides may read. History not only moved on the old Natchez Trace; on its parkway now people are hurrying to history with all their boys and girls in tow. The prettiest girls now wear costumes as they guide all comers to history. He is a poor chamber of commerce secretary who does not know local history as well as labor statistics. History has become a cash crop as eagerly tended as the hope for industrial plants.

Certainly none should welcome this new interest more than such men as yourselves. Polish the antiques. Plant the grass around the forts where the Indians sought—and often got—the scalps. Tend the graves of the statesmen. Mark the streets and roads to the houses where grace and greatness dwelt.

But all this is façade. Behind it the task is still the industrious, often the drudging collection of the little details of local history which are the only components of the history of mankind.

Collectors and evaluators of such details are the only important people still in the keeping—and the keeping straight—of our heritage. And only such men can hope to understand at last what history is. I doubt that there will be any pat answers like those about what is news. But the quest is yours. I salute your studies as I hope to snatch from them.

Some other researchers may tell us how to get to the moon. Your greater task is to help us put together the basis for understanding: what is man. We can only hope to understand that on the ground, on the scene, in the localities, there man acted in the past and there he acts in the news and history he is making now for tomorrow morning's paper and for the reservoirs of records for all time.

The newsman and the history man work on the same beat. And life is a local story. God grant that we may serve it well!

What's New and Effective In Museum Interpretation?

Introduction

Frederick L. Rath, Jr.

No one knows how far back in the dim shadows of time man first displayed for public benefit a work of art, a piece of prized material, or an ancient object. Nor can anyone point clearly to the setting up of the first museum—literally, the seat of the Muses. What we do know is that the movement so long a-borning is today undergoing a spectacular revolution, especially in the United States. During this century alone literally thousands of museums of all kinds—art, natural science, history, industrial—as well as historic houses, restored or reconstructed and period-furnished, and historic sites have been established and opened to the public. And to them each year are flocking well over a hundred million visitors.

The result is a kind of revolution in presentation techniques. Once it was enough simply to sort, classify, and then hang or lay out in cases of every description materials and objects, scientific, artistic, or historical. But now presentation or display has itself become both an art and a science.

Today the materials of a collection are used not so much for random, desultory display as for educational purposes. The magic word now is *interpretation,* especially in historical displays and history museums. Even as a professor of history analyzes and selects his evidence for verbal or written presentation, interpreters in the historic preservation field use a carefully selected grouping of three-dimensional materials for their presentation. I have come to think of interpretation as inspired revelation, based on sound scholarship and designed to make people think for themselves about meanings and ideas and relationships, past and present.

Presenting historical materials artfully has itself resulted in some long, hard thoughts. Throughout the country today members of museum staffs are experimenting with presentation techniques, the more expert handling of museum materials for educational purposes.

At its annual meeting in Raleigh, North Carolina, in the fall of 1963, the American Association for State and Local History scheduled a session entitled "What's New and Effective in Interpretation?". Obviously, in a relatively short session, only a limited number of the innumerable facets of interpretation could be presented, but each of the experienced professionals who presented papers had something to say and said it well. It was a stimulating session, and since the texts were in hand it was decided that others might be stimulated by reading them. May you, the reader, profit from these thoughts as we, the listeners, did last fall.

Natural Light and the Museum

Wilcomb E. Washburn

Is natural light obsolete for museum purposes? When I hear the frequent and confident assertion that it is obsolete, my gorge rises almost as much as when I hear paeans of praise for a modern, flexible, "twentieth-century" all-bus system advocated as superior to an out-moded, "nineteenth-century" rail system in handling the problem of the movement of people in the modern American city.

The confidence with which museum directors and designers have dismissed natural light from their thinking reflects, to some degree, Western Man's constant challenging of Nature and his cultural indisposition to accommodate himself to it. The faith in the ability of man to outdo nature in the field of lighting is well expressed in *Light, Vision and Seeing: A Simplified Presentation of Their Relationships and Their Importance in Human Efficiency and Welfare,* by Matthew Luckiesh, Director, Lighting Research Laboratory, General Electric Company, Nela Park, Cleveland, a book published in 1944 (New York: D. Van Nostrand Company, Inc.). In a section entitled "Challenging the Sun," Mr. Luckiesh, in a typical passage discussing the increasing efficiency of lamps, writes: "But this is not the end. By following Nature's textbook we shall duplicate the good features of Nature's light and lighting. And that is not the end. We shall improve upon Nature by applying light and lighting specifically for our artificial world. Still this is not the end."

In a conference of museum and gallery directors on the subject of Planning Museums and Art Galleries, held in Bristol, England, in 1962, J. B. Harris, of the Ministry of Public Buildings and Works, questioned "whether any advantage can be gained by trying to use natural lighting as a working illumination," and quoted approvingly the architect Sir Hugh Casson's talk at the Museums Association Conference in 1961 to the effect that, "It may be wiser to exclude daylight completely so that the strictest control can be kept over the lighting of the exhibits and real daylight should be used only occasionally for the visual relief of visitors who might otherwise feel uncomfortable if shut off from the world outside."

Design specialists, as might be expected, are the most outspoken in ignoring or condemning natural light. For example, James Gardner and Caroline Heller, in their book *Exhibition and Display* (New York: F. W. Dodge Corporation, 1960), assert that "Daylight is rarely satisfactory as exhibition lighting: it is too temperamental in cold climates and too brilliant in tropical climates; in any climate it changes direction and quality throughout the day. If there is any choice in the matter, it is really desirable from a display point of view to have a building with no windows so that all illumination is under control."

I would like to enter a dissent from this prevailing view concerning the inability of natural light to serve museum purposes as well or better than artificial lighting. My discussion will be in part theoretical, and in part based on practical examples. It is possible to achieve ideal lighting of specific objects at specific places under either natural or artificial conditions, but too often the practice falls far short of the ideal. Since, in my view, too little thought has been given to creating ideal natural lighting conditions for museums, and too little note has been taken of faults in the use of artificial lighting, I shall concern myself in this paper primarily with those two aspects of the matter.

First of all, I feel that the current trend to shut out natural light is illustrative of one of the great failures of much of our modern architecture: to wit, the failure to relate buildings to their environment. This problem has been discussed at length by such architectural leaders as Paul Rudolph. Its terrifying implications have been argued persuasively by such city planners as Constantinos Doxiadis. The museum architect has, in particular, I think, failed to relate the process of object-viewing in museums to the environment of natural light with which man is blessed. The reasons for this reluctance to use natural light are many and I shall go into some in the course of this paper. Cost and performance factors, based on existing technological knowledge, seem to force the architect into this position, but much of the problem, as I see it, is caused by the architect's willingness to capitulate to such conditions and his unwillingness to seek alternatives that could relate the natural environment efficiently to the lighting requirements of the museum.

The fault, or virtue, of excluding natural light from the museum must rest with the museum director as well as with the architect and his lighting and design consultants. Perhaps the director simply accepts the advice of his architect. Perhaps he positively demands a light system that he can control with precision. Perhaps he relishes a system which allows him to create attention-getting "effects" more easily than with natural light.

Recently, in Norfolk, I observed a painting by Dorothy Greenberg (in the Alfred Khouri Memorial Collection) which had been done with the vigorous strokes and heavy paint accumulations of some of the modern school. At one point on the painting, which was entitled "Eden," paint projected one quarter of an inch. The lighting—artificial—was provided by high-powered spots from above and close to the canvas, a manner of lighting consistent throughout the room. The result was the creation of a series of secondary areas of varying shapes and colors, created in the shaded portions under the variously projecting bits of paint. I wondered whether the lighting had been consciously arranged to comprehend the resulting canvas, but concluded that it had not. Yet here was a new painting, in effect created by the placement and intensity of the lights, which could be varied at will by shifting the locations and varying the intensities (why not the color) of the lights. Admittedly, this is an extreme example, but I cite it to show the positive role played by the museum lighting man and to illustrate my point that the museum director may unwittingly or consciously manipulate and create, rather than carefully place and show in a manner least calculated to violate their original essence, the objects in his custody.

The museum director who fancies himself an impressario tends to demonstrate his control both of the dead artist and of the living sun by his manipulation of statuary. It is possible to create dramatic highlights and shadows on even the most pedestrian sculpture and to give effects that do not exist in the clear unspotted light of day. Compare, for example, the appearance of mid-nineteenth century romantic American sculpture, much of it produced in Italy, much of it glorying in its smooth, snow-white finish, in a dark corridor under the glare of ceiling spot lights, and, by interest, in a gallery off an open courtyard. Such sculpture was meant to be seen under conditions approximating the latter example, not the first. Yet one finds, too frequently, that just the opposite practice prevails.

I suspect that much of the preference for artificial light is not only the result of the specific advantages it seems to convey, but also because of the willingness of architects, museum directors, and design men, to follow practices in other seemingly related fields. Too often, in my opinion, those concerned with constructing museums have merely adapted techniques of lighting and display developed for other—usually commercial—purposes, without realizing that these techniques are frequently inappropriate to the purpose of a museum. Sometimes museum displays have merely introduced used-car dealer or department store lighting. The high-powered, "point" lighting of a used-car dealer's lot has its own purposes: to sell second-hand cars, particularly at night, to an audience which is often dazzled by the sparkling reflection from point sources of light on highly polished automobile chassis. Museum goers should be as suspicious of a museum director who uses light for special effects—unless they can be justified for valid reasons—as car buyers should be wary of a high-powered used-car dealer.

In like fashion, department stores have special requirements in their lighting problems, both from a lack of natural light available, and from a desire to put the best "light" on a piece of goods in order to sell it. Because department stores are customarily in crowded town centers, are multi-storied, and appeal to night-time shoppers, they need artificial lighting both inside and outside.

A museum, on the other hand, is often a one- or two-story building, and is often located in an area that is free from nearby buildings that block access to natural light. Moreover, it is normally open only during the daylight hours. Is it really necessary to ignore, or positively shut out, the natural light available? We are all aware, of course, of the destructive nature of light on most classes of museum objects.

We are also all aware of the space-consuming, expensive, inadequate, and, indeed, nerve-wracking qualities of existing technology for receiving and distributing natural light within a museum. Laurence Vail Coleman, in his *Museum Buildings:* Volume One: *A Planning Study* (Washington: American Association of Museums, 1950) has given an excellent summary of the strengths and defects of existing natural lighting systems. But is it not a confession of failure, or at least acceptance of existing architectural conventions, to eliminate natural light because it requires greater effort to control than artificial light? Why cannot natural light be controlled as effectively as artificial light and at the same time provide more, better, safer, and cheaper light? A modern building need not allow natural light to stream through windows or skylights with only curtains, blinds, or filters of one sort or another, to control, direct, and diffuse the light.

What are the requirements of an ideal natural lighting system for a museum? Are these ideals attainable? Natural light should be as available in a museum as water from a faucet or cool air from a duct. It should be capable of being introduced into the viewing area from above, behind, and from each side of the viewer in varying proportions depending upon the object being viewed and the wishes of the curator. It should be capable of being regulated in intensity, but allowed to vary in intensity in accordance with the nature of the material being lighted and the aesthetic principles of the curator in charge. It should be so diffused and so directed to the object that glare and reflection are minimized. Finally, it should be capable of being redirected with exhibit changes.

Let us consider whether and how these specifications can be met.

Since the outer walls of a building provide the largest area of display space, let us consider a scheme to utilize the outer walls, rather than movable floor panels, or the inner walls of a building unit, for exhibit purposes under natural light. To simplify the discussion, let us consider a single box-type display unit, which might be an entire small museum or a cellular unit of a larger museum.

The light can be introduced in a conventional fashion by designing a courtyard within the display unit and constructing windows and/or a skylight to allow for the entrance of light. But let us see if we cannot devise a more efficient means of directing the light, even if two or more such units are on top of each other.

I would suggest that the light available can be captured by a series of reflectors, both above and within the unit, which can transmit a higher proportion of light than will fall naturally into such an area, directly onto the exhibit surfaces from positions appropriate to the different objects to be lighted. By allowing for the shifting of the reflectors, the light, whether from the early morning sun or late afternoon sun, or general overcast, can be directed to the display area of any of the four walls of the exhibit unit in equal or varying amount. It is not inconceivable that lenses to focus the light can have a place in the scheme, particularly where units are "stacked" one above the other.

In the course of writing this paper, I had occasion to discuss my requirements for piping in light with Mr. Carroll B. Lusk, a lighting specialist at the Smithsonian Institution. He suggested that something might be done with rod-type ducting, such as is used in one or two internal surgical instruments. Light can be made to reflect totally as it passes through a plexiglass rod even though the rod is bent to a certain maximum radius. By this means, light could be carried to almost any part of a building if it could be directed into the rod from a central source, or, indeed, from multiple sources. Shortly after our discussion, Mr. Lusk received the September, 1963, issue of the *Lucite Spectrum,* (Vol. 1, No. 2), a trade publication concerning du Pont Lucite acrylic plastic materials, which featured the results of a 1963 competition sponsored by du Pont at the Yale University School of Art and Architecture. Creative design utilizing Lucite was the basic criterion for the selection of the award winners, and though none used a completely commercially available set of components, the judges felt that all were distinctly within the realm of possibility. One design, that of David Wright, uses a reflecting lens and rods of Lucite acrylic resin to conduct piped natural sunlight throughout a low-rise building. Effective transmission of light is proportional to the distance over which the light is conducted and is, hence, a limiting factor. An unusual "light collector" focuses as much light as possible on the head of the light-conducting rod. A similar component picks up the light from the conducting rod and redistributes it about a room not otherwise open to daylight.

Wright's plan is an example of the imaginative thinking that needs to be considered by architects and museum theorists. I am shocked when I see that the means of controlling natural light have still not progressed much beyond the devices used in the Renaissance and earlier. Venetian blinds and fine mesh cloth are still the principal means of controlling natural light in museums, with various forms of tinted and treated glass playing an increasing, though inflexible, role.

Of course many new museums have adapted natural light with great efficiency. Outstanding in this regard is the Municipal Museum of Amsterdam, the Stedelijk, whose two-story new wing devoted to temporary exhibits, constructed about 1954, is in the form of a box with glass walls. The exhibits are mounted on movable panels standing in the floor area. Natural light floods the exhibit areas and can be controlled by ceiling to floor blinds. A French critic, writing in 1956, said that he did not believe that there was an exposition hall in the entire world more ideal, or better adapted to the modern spirit and to the flexible use of space.

The reconstruction of the Museum of Capodimonte, Naples, Italy, following its damage in World War II, is another triumph in the imaginative use of natural light. Glass skylights were inserted in the roof, and the light controlled and diffused prior to its admission into the upper galleries.

Nevertheless, both museums do little more than admit natural light directly into the viewing areas, with simple methods of reducing the intensity of the light.

Some museums under construction may be demonstrating a way to control natural light more effectively than it has been controlled in the past. Luis Sert's art museum for Aime Maeght near Saint-Paul-de-Vence, on the Côte d'Azur in France, may be one of these.

I cannot express similar satisfaction with other contemporary efforts in Europe. The "Greek and Roman Life" room at the British Museum has utilized artificial light in the skylight, plus numerous internally lighted cases. The results are disconcerting. There are many disturbing highlights and dark spots. The glare and reflection problem in several of the cases is serious.

The Kestner Museum, in Hanover, Germany, imaginatively incorporated into its new structure the façade of its old bombed-out predecessor. But its handling of light, both artificial and natural, varies from outstanding to atrocious. In some galleries, natural light is admitted through glass domes on top of the building which can be opened to allow a sight of the sky. These domes throw a changing natural light on the classical sculpture and ceramics in the galleries. But one can often find oneself eyeball to eyeball with a dropped spot light, unnecessarily competing with the sun, or, in other parts of the museum, hardly perceive Roman busts because of the strong back lighting from uncontrolled window openings.

It may well be that history and technology museums can utilize artificial light without violating the integrity of the utilitarian objects on display. But I wonder if this is possible for an art museum or any museum where the light in which the object was made is inextricably intertwined in the aesthetic theory with which it is viewed. What we need to know is not alone the number of foot candles thrown on the object. What we need is a measure of the glare—both disability glare and discomfort glare—that interferes with the ease of viewing the object; a scale of distortion, indicated in terms of depth of shadow and sharpness of contrast caused by directional light from an agreed-upon norm based on general light of an agreed-upon character obtained out of doors; a measure of the perceived dullness of nearby objects less brilliantly lighted; in sum, measures that will help us determine the extent to which our aesthetic pleasure in, or rational comprehension of an object is affected by the lighting it receives.

Let us take a simple example of the effect of lighting one painting in an art gallery without lighting nearby paintings. When the National Gallery of Art received *La Liseuse* by Fragonard it placed it for temporary exhibition upon a panel under several spot lights. The painting glowed under the treatment. The rich yellows, particularly, stood out. Paintings in adjoining halls, lacking equivalent light, however, seemed lifeless when compared directly with *Le Liseuse*.

One of the strongest apparent reasons for replacing natural lighting systems with artificial systems is that on particularly dark days natural light is insufficient to give a proper illumination to many objects on display. This was the principal reason natural light was completely eliminated in the recent renovation of the Hall of Life in the Sea and in the Hall of Dinosaurs and Other Reptiles of the Natural History Building of the Smithsonian Institution. In the one case, the natural light that formerly came in from the skylight was replaced with artificial lights, giving off a pale bluish color, but coming from the same position and giving a generalized illumination to the hall. In the other hall, an attempt has been made to illuminate the major specimens with directional lighting from above while keeping the area above the displays unlighted and the viewing areas comparatively so. Neither of the two halls seems satisfactory to me, although they please others. The "coolness" of the Whale Hall which was sought by the designers, seems dead to me and, indeed in the words of one friend, "sick". Our negative opinions are personal, of course, and many other friends praise the new lighting highly. The blue glow may help the viewer get below the surface with the plunging whale, but he instinctively feels that he wishes to get out and rise to the sunlit surface. Whether the process of learning is enhanced by one or the other type of lighting is a matter for the psychologists to decide. I am also curious as to whether the new lighting tends to attract or repel visitors. I have not noted many people staying for long periods in the hall. This may partly be because the entire exhibit is not yet finished. But the discomfort I feel in the hall makes me hesitate to stay long enough to be entertained or educated.

Applied to an art museum the loss of natural lighting is even more serious. I am informed that the John and Mable Ringling Museum of Art in Sarasota is in the process of having its windows walled up and its light sources cut off in order to allow for the installation of air conditioning. Air conditioning is fine for both paintings and visitor, but is it a value to take precedence over natural light? I have detailed some of the tests by which I believe the quality of light in a museum should be judged. But there is an even more important value that is sacrificed when one excludes natural light. That is, the infinite variety of natural light in all its moods, from blazing, summer, noon-day sun, to gloomy, winter, stormy day. I realize that this variety which I cherish is regarded as a menace by engineers. Perhaps the engineers can convince us that an artificial system will be preferable to certain natural conditions, such as excessive sunlight or excessive gloom, but let us not forget that this normally means exchanging variety for consistency. We are doomed to miss the exaltation of seeing Van Gogh's painting *Wheatfield with Reaper,* for example, in the sky-lighted gallery of the main building of the Stedelijk Museum in Amsterdam, suddenly and subtly change with the appearance and reappearance of the sun through the clouds of Holland. Should the viewer be content with a consistent artificial light, whatever its spectral composition, provided by an engineer or museum director for seeing this painting? Perhaps, but I would prefer to see how the painting changes under the natural light under which Van Gogh worked.

One of the most basic human instincts is the desire to avoid being shut away from the natural environment. Lighting engineers, peeved by this perverse elemental reaction against their neat schemes, have tried to solve the problem by leaving glimpses of natural light in corners, at one end of a gallery, or elsewhere. They speak of the necessity to give "relief" to the visitor and a sense of the possibility of "escape" from the ideal world they have constructed for him. If the human instinct to escape from such a world is so strong, may it not be that the world is not so ideal after all? It would be an interesting experiment to determine whether piped-in natural light in an enclosed space satisfies the primal urge of man for a relationship with nature, or whether he will have the same dissatisfaction evident under artificial lighting conditions. The museum must create the feeling of relationship to life rather than to death. That relationship requires an elemental connection with the sun, the source of all life. The museum builder can ignore this primal urge only at his peril. A mausoleum is still a mausoleum, no matter how many lights have been placed in it.

Of course, I do not exclude a proper "mix" of artificial and natural light. Given the inadequacies of existing technologies, given the variability of the seasonal conditions, it is often not only a necessary but an ideal solution to use such a mix. Many a practical museum man is delighted to use both, whatever his philosophical predispositions concerning the theoretical superiority of daylight or artificial light. I am perfectly prepared to accept artificial lighting when natural light falls below a certain minimum intensity, for example. However, for the purposes of theoretical clarity in this discussion, I have isolated natural and artificial components of light.

The American concern with "packaging" is as evident in the American museum world as it is in the commercial world. Gleaming, aluminum-framed cases, blazing lights, rich fabric backgrounds, polished, fine-grained wood bases, are symbols of the American devotion to the need to impress and to attract a viewer by the outer form as well as by the inner substance. Such concern with "packaging" need not be condemned outright. Sometimes it gives life to a collection or to an object which was "dead". But this concern can also result in the object being eclipsed in the glory of the package.

It is instructive to note that those countries having the greatest museum treasures and the longest artistic traditions feel least compelled to dress up their objects. One can learn much from the museums in Greece, for example, whether he visits the National Museum in Athens, or a small museum such as that at Argos. He will perhaps be unable to find any electric lights or novel display arrangements. But he will see the objects that form such an important part of our cultural heritage, and he will see them well.

The essence of museum presentation is to have a cultural object to see (not to have a "product" to "sell") and to be able to see it well, clearly, without distortion, and with the aesthetic pleasure or intellectual understanding which the object demands. Too often our museums have fallen into display clichés in presenting the objects they possess. Worse, they are other people's clichés. The museum has purposes different from the private dwelling, the commercial office building, or the department store. Yet it has too often been repeating the lighting and display clichés, to say nothing of the architectural form, of these other institutions.

It is time for the museum to be redesigned from the inside out, without reference to the past or the present. I venture to predict that museums can be built that display more objects better and cheaper than any now existing. The museum has two great assets to begin with: the objects and the natural light to illuminate them. I think they should be brought together.

Devices as Aids to Interpretation

Harold L. Peterson

When Wilcomb Washburn first asked me to present a paper to this august gathering, I was flattered. When he told me the subject, I was dismayed. What is new and effective in interpretation? Right away we are dealing with two very difficult concepts. Effectiveness is especially elusive. Most of us judge it by our own reactions and what we think are those of visitors, perhaps what we think the reactions of visitors ought to be. We have very few scientific tests that reveal effectiveness in any completely satisfactory manner. My comments on this subject, therefore, must be made in terms of what I think personally. An effective device, to me, is one that I think works well. An ineffective device is one that does not appeal to me.

Newness is also difficult. There are very few things that have never been tried before in some form or another. The best we can look for is a new application or a modification of a known principle. With this in mind, I have selected a few activities and enterprises, that to me at least, seem to have something new and different about them.

One of the first areas of endeavor to which one turns when he seeks to find a new interpretive device is the world of electronics. Here at least one does not have to trace interpretive theory back so many years to look for possible precedents. It is a new science. It is modern and in tune with today's world. Thus I believe that it offers several things for us to consider.

One of the major electronic attempts at interpretation in recent years is the sound and light program. Almost everyone is familiar with these productions in which recorded voices, sound effects, and music are combined with lighting to dramatize historic events associated with buildings, ships, or even fields. Many of you, perhaps, have seen this technique employed at Versailles, at the Chateaux in the Loire Valley, at the Tower of London, at *HMS Victory* or one of the other notable installations in Europe.

Following these successes abroad, it was only natural that sound and light should be proposed for the United States. The National Park Service has received many proposals for initiating such programs in both historical and natural parks. These proposals caused grave soul searching and much study. Sound and Light programs do not spring full blown from the undisturbed earth. They require the installation of equipment. There must be towers for the lights, columns for the speakers, seats for the audience, comfort facilities, housing for the control system, cables, wiring, and a host of other impedimenta—all of which have an effect on the historic building or ground. Most of the proposals were rejected outright, but two areas were selected for experimental programs where conditions seemed most appropriate. These were the Castillo de San Marcos National Monument at St. Augustine, Florida, and Independence Hall at Philadelphia, Pennsylvania. Here it was felt the installations could be effected with the least intrusion on the historic scene. At the same time, they offered the desiderata of proximity to a metropolitan center and therefore to a large number of visitors who would be remaining overnight. In both cases the installation and productions were provided by private corporations under a concessions agreement with the U. S. Government. They were fully professional from the engineers and script writers to the actors who included such well-known personalities as Fredric March. Production expenses were great.

This past summer has marked the second season of operation for both these programs. To put it mildly, the audience response has been disappointing—especially to the investors who financed the operations. Crowds the second summer have been smaller than the first. Many causes have been suggested for this failure to attract the public. They range from the type of material employed, to the dramatic productions themselves, the physical surroundings, and the climate of public opinion. Few of the experts have agreed upon the proper cause or causes. All agree that thus far sound and light in America, or at least in these two instances, has not been successful.

By contrast, there is one new electronic method which we do consider outstandingly effective. It is not a brand new approach, but we believe there are new features about it. Those of us who have had any connection with it are highly enthusiastic, and the public response we have received has been equally so. This is the use of audio phones for interpreting historic houses. Audio devices have been used before in many variations with which I am sure you are familiar. Some of them are broadcast types offering a choice of two or three different programs. Some use telephone jacks that the visitor can plug in as he stands before an exhibit. Always before, to our knowledge, however, they have been used for formal museum installations.

The application of which I speak offers three variations: first, it is the interpretation of an historic house rather than a museum exhibit; second, the type of audio unit itself is new; and third, the narration is provided by an actual resident of the house during its historic period.

The installation of which I speak is at the Home of Franklin D. Roosevelt National Memorial. The units are Acoustiguide tape repeaters. Each one is an individual tape recorder which is carried in a bag slung over the shoulder with either one or two earpieces so that a couple may share the same instrument. The operator has control over volume and can start and stop the machine at will. The recording itself is timed so that the visitor may leave it on and walk from room to room. If he desires to remain in a location after a description has been given, however, he simply turns off the machine and starts it again when he is ready for the next stop on his tour. This gives ample freedom for the most studious visitor to examine any detail to his heart's content. These machines provide superior fidelity, and since they are self-contained with their own tapes, there is no static or interference of any kind. If there is a mechanical failure of any kind, it affects one unit only. It cannot disrupt the entire program. The Corning Glass Museum and the Los Angeles County Museum also employ this particular device.

We believe that such devices are of great assistance in interpreting historic houses, but this one has a further distinction. The voice and narration were provided by the late Eleanor Roosevelt herself. The recording was made as she walked from room to room through the house telling what she knew about it, pointing out pieces of furniture, and adding anecdotes and stories of human interest. The sensation of hearing a well-known voice in high fidelity talk about a home in which its owner was hostess for many years offers the visitor a personal experience that can seldom be equalled.

These have been two experiences with electronic interpretation which have seemed to be new or have new facets. From these, I would like to go one step further and discuss other possible uses of electronic interpretation which have not yet been tried. They should at least have the virtue of being new—unless I learn this morning that some of you have already experimented along these lines and are way ahead of me.

First, I should like to suggest that sound is an important element in the creation of a mood. There are certain sounds that everyone associates with a building or an activity, and if one does not hear these sounds, the illusion of authenticity is seriously affected. Sometimes these may be noises of which the hearer is conscious. Sometimes they may be subliminal. I wonder if it would not aid greatly to add some of these sounds to our historic settings to help recreate an historic—or at least a nostalgic—atmosphere.

This, of course, could be easily overdone. The noises of conflict on a battlefield would be out of place because they would obviously be false and probably in bad taste as well. I am thinking more of simple sounds which are keyed to a building or site and which one can hear without automatically looking for the person, animal, or object producing the sound. Church bells would be a good example. The visitor could hear the call to Matins, Evensong, Vespers, or other services of the day rung as they would have been at the time. The pealing of church bells adds a distinct nostalgic mood to a recreated village. The same would be true of ship bells. Anyone who has had experience aboard ship knows that the distinct sound of a ship's bell striking every 15 minutes is an essential aspect of any vessel in active duty. It can be heard throughout much of the ship, and it quickly suggests life.

The National Park Service plans to conduct an experiment along these lines among the western forts and posts which it administers. We have selected the sound of bugle calls. Elizabeth Custer, in writing of her life at the western forts, mentions the sound of the bugle as one of her clearest recollections of fort life and activity. "It was the hourly monitor. . . . ," she wrote. "It told us when to eat, to sleep, to march, and to go to church. . . . We needed time pieces only when absent from garrison or camp. The never tardy sound calling to duty was better than any clock and brought us up standing; and instead of the usual remark, 'Why here it is four o'clock already!' We found ourselves saying: 'Can it be possible? There's "stables," and where has the day gone?' "

The National Park Service has recorded the daily series of these bugle calls using a contemporary instrument, and we hope soon to use this tape at Fort Davis with a timed player and loudspeaker so that the proper calls will sound out over the parade ground at the proper time each day. We feel that this will add one more dimension to the visitor's experience at the Fort, offering instruction, some aesthetic pleasure from the simple melodies, and perhaps a pleasant nostalgia. If this attempt proves successful, we shall try it at other posts— at least those which are well preserved, and in which the buildings still stand. We are not sure what the effect would be if this were tried at a post in ruins such as Fort Union. But this, too, might be a very worthwhile experiment.

The church bells, the ship bells, and the army bugle are a few of the sounds that come to mind immediately when one thinks of this appeal to the auditory sense in interpretation. There are many more, and I think they might offer a field worthy of exploration.

The sound and light program, the use of the Acoustiguide in historic houses, the experiments in appealing to the visitor's auditory sense as well as his vision are electronic activities in the field of interpretation which are, I hope, new. There are many other uses of electronics—the talking label is familiar to all of us. There are frequent proposals to install some two-way telephone sets in front of exhibits through which a visitor could converse with an interpreter in a central location, ask questions, and receive answers so that one staff member could offer information to a visitor no matter where he was in an area. And there are a multitude of similar suggestions by which one is offered a saving in interpretive manpower by substituting a mechanical gadget.

Here, I think, is a danger. Certainly it is better to offer mechanical information than none at all. But is it better, given the choice, than a live interpreter? There may be some cases in which it is, but the question of where, when, and how to exploit its advantages without becoming cold and impersonal is a question that all of us must meet as we ask, "Is it new and effective?"

Approaches to Interpretation

Robert B. Inverarity

It occurs to me that most people who attend meetings of this sort do so, either to meet new people or renew old acquaintances, or to acquire some bit of knowledge which will help them in their work. To the first group there is little that I can contribute and to the second group I must confess there is no magic potion nor words of wisdom that I may speak. Although I shall use the word "museum" constantly, what I have to say, I believe, applies equally well in many instances to other similar institutions such as historical societies and art galleries. I am going to talk around, not about, installations and interpretations because I am not convinced there is very much new in these areas.

Museums are different and hence, although there are many basic similarities, the differences are part of their uniqueness and one of their reasons for being. The proliferation of museums in America is almost unbelievable—it has been said that at least one new museum opens each week—and if we are to continue at this rate, we shall have more museums than material to go in them. A great desire exists to develop new museums rather than to consider the need, resources, and what a new museum may hope to offer. In other words, museums may have become a status symbol—such as a Rolls Royce—so if your community does not have a museum, it is obviously an uncultured town. I am sorry to see the development of this type of thinking. Perhaps it has always been with us and I am only now becoming aware of this point of view.

To discuss interpretation, without considering the museum, is as if in medicine one attempted to study only the foot. One cannot amputate a foot, place it on a pedestal, and study it successfully because the weight of the body, the use to which the foot is put, the blood supply, the connecting muscles and tendons and other factors all have a bearing on this appendage. Likewise a museum has a relationship to a country and community. The amount of funds available, the physical plant, the philosophy of its program, and the staff, all of these go to make up the kind of interpretation which can be attempted and what exhibits the museum will display.

Then there is also the important element of just what collections the museum may have, or can borrow, for exhibition. All of these factors have something to do with what the public may see and how successfully the institution has done its job.

The starting point of an exhibition is obviously an idea or object. Either approach can result in the same exhibition. The exhibition which starts with an idea must be composed of objects which in some way, when grouped together, convey the idea to the visitor. The exhibition which starts with the object may, or may not, achieve the same result. The object does not change very much with the passage of time, other than possibly to develop a patina or to deteriorate. Therefore, over a long period of time, collections of objects have been made and placed on exhibition in no organized manner. Most of us are familiar with such exhibitions—they are too numerous. It is important that objects be saved by collecting, but a collection of objects saved and stored in cases for public view is not a successful exhibition. Often there is a confusion between storage areas and exhibition areas, and too many museum people have stored their collections in exhibition cases and attempted to keep all of their collections on view.

The keynote is the frame of reference.

Twenty Tarascan figures can be placed in a case and exhibited; this is a collection of Tarascan figures—in other words, a group of objects. This display has value to the specialist. There is little consideration for lighting, color, texture, labels, theme, or anything else, simply an arrangement of objects. However, with judgment and taste, it is possible to remove a few of the finest Tarascan figures from this group, separate them, and light them well. When this is done, they can be viewed as objects of art. Perhaps the group of figures can be arranged in a particular sequence to show a change in style or chronology. The group can be mixed with other objects to give a flavor of the culture. The figures might be so arranged as to illustrate the technique of producing this sculpture, or a phase of the technology of the culture. A selection might be made which would illustrate the everyday life and pursuits of the Tarascan people. It all depends on what you are trying to do and what is the frame of reference. A painting, if of good enough quality, can simply be displayed by itself as a work of art. It can be included in a group show of the artist's works, or a group show of other artists of the same period. It can be included with other paintings to show a sequence in the development of painting, or it may be grouped with other paintings to show a way of life at a certain time. It can be placed in a period room as one element in recreating the atmosphere of an environment, where as an object it is one among many to develop a unified effect. In all this, the object, whether it be a Tarascan figure or a painting, has not changed— what has changed is the frame of reference.

The frame of reference can be defined by other means but I find it a good term to assist in visualizing the problem. Lacking a frame of reference is the same as lacking a belt for your trousers. If you are big enough, it makes no difference, as the trousers will fit snugly and stay up. But if you are thin, you will either lose your trousers or spend a fair amount of time trying to hold them up. The large, portly museum can exhibit anything it wishes. Due to its prestige and size it can get away with it. The small, lean, or new museum had best beware. If it tries the same thing, a large amount of time will be spent in trying to justify such an exhibition.

I mentioned earlier that one cannot discuss interpretation without discussing other factors which are important and aid in shaping the exhibition and its frame of reference. Truly, I am astonished at how successful certain individuals and institutions have become with their attitude of "Let's do another show quickly and tell 'em it's great." We are fast becoming addicted to the cult of numbers and verbiage. The cult of numbers is one which says, "Because my institution has 300,000 visitors a year it is better than yours which has only 20,000 visitors a year. We put on twelve shows last year while you only did six—so obviously we are a better museum." This is insanity. Because you do a survey of visitor reactions and out of a hundred samplings seventy-five of them say you should have more early fire engines on exhibit, are you going out and buy early fire engines like mad? First of all, perhaps there was a convention of fire chiefs in your town during the time the survey was taken and you didn't know about it! Secondly, don't fall for the old ploy—that the majority is always right. If we start to judge our work and institution by the numbers or values of the majority, we most likely should be doing some other kind of work and we most likely have few values of our own. It is time that more people in the museum field stop settling for what is expedient and pleases the great tasteless horde—how in the world will the public develop taste if the museums do not take a stand? Are we merchandising art and history, and will we only stock what the public will buy? Should a historical society throw out everything in its manuscript collections that has not been used at least once a year or once every five years? If this form of thinking is to prevail, Lord help the historical collections of America.

This type of thinking may be found on both sides of the situation, as witnessed by the board of directors, trustees, municipal authorities, and so forth, who evaluate the amount of money devoted to an institution by its public use. Pity the poor staff caught between the administration and the public, both with the attitude of quantity, let quality fall where it may. The staff is then in an untenable position. Too many people continue to suffer in such a schizophrenic situation because, if they voice their opinions, it will mean losing their jobs and retirement pay. I hope the development of new museums will help these people find other positions.

You may remember I suggested earlier our addiction to verbiage as well as numbers. Too many times I am subjected to the advertising approach when I read museum literature. How many times have you read a glowing account in an institution's folder only to find on first-hand inspection that the words actually have little relation to the facts? Or meet the person who always reports on every place he visits with nothing but praise? As individuals many of us are afraid of being unpopular if we voice anything but "soft soap." The popular fellow is the one who says everything is absolutely wonderful and is everlastingly all things to all people. I am sure you would much prefer to have me stand here and tell you how wonderful we all are but, you know, I don't think we all are wonderful. I do think there are many superb institutions in America that have great material and produce outstanding exhibitions. But I would enter a plea for a bit more honesty in our judgments. By this I do not suggest we let loose a vindictive avalanche of words. I do propose that by thoughtful, honest suggestions we place high regard on our own value judgments. In turn, the verbalizing we do regarding our own work and institutions might then reflect a more factual picture. However, if great popular acclaim and numbers of visitors are what you wish, the formula for this is well known.

Witness the commercial enterprises fast developing in America called "attractions". Take a page out of their book and follow the gang to Disneyland. If you have an outdoor museum, get a little

train the kids can ride on, or a stagecoach that is held up on a
regular schedule. If you have a general museum, I guarantee that
Jivaro heads and a mummy or two will help magnetize your
institution. You have an art museum—well, that's not too difficult.
Simply pay an outrageous price for a painting and the public will
flock to the doors to have a three-second glance before they are
pushed on by other eager, money-conscious lookers. If you have a
history museum, I would suppose one or two of George Washington's beds would help.

Some museums and "attractions" are on a collision course—they
are converging. "Attractions" are using objects which should be in
museums to "dress-up" their activities. One county fair which I
occasionally see has a superb, early, steam locomotive which should
be preserved in a museum but which is slowly deteriorating as an
outdoor display piece. Likewise museums are borrowing from "attractions" some of their glamour techniques. Unless we each
attempt to define clearly in our own minds what we are trying to
do, the way to do it will constantly be in danger of turning into
confusion. Only by developing this skeleton can the viscera of
exhibitions and interpretation hang solid.

I support the thesis that museums are unique and that they can
present to their visitors an experience which is not attainable elsewhere. It is this quality which we must search for in our work
and interpretations.

One pitfall which can be easily escaped, if recognized, is the
tendency to produce an exhibition which should be done in some
other medium. Certain themes are better developed in writing,
a photobook, a motion picture, or some other means than an exhibition.

I am a believer in attempting to find your own way of doing
things. Surely we are not making a contribution to our own institutions, or to the cultural world in general, if we merely develop a
composite interpretation of what we have seen in a number of
other places. I have written before of the dubious value of the visitor
seeing the same little schoolhouse exhibition repeated in one museum after another. There are fashions in exhibitions, as in everything else, and it is a normal failing to desire to be in style and
therefore a part of the crowd. But if everyone is dressed in khaki,
what a monotonous aspect! I would hope that each of us can in
some way enhance the uniqueness of the material we exhibit by the

manner and interpretation of how we do it. This is not to say that because new materials and techniques are becoming available to us we need use every possible device. The overstressing of the exhibition technique may only confuse the viewer. The animated, chromium, colorful, flashing, buzzing, pinball machine need not be transplanted into the gallery. If it is, the viewer may remember a startling exhibition but have no idea of what it was all about. This is "exhibition of confusion."

All museums and exhibitions need not be great. There will always be a vast range of levels of achievement and this is as it should be. One beautifully done room can be a joy to behold and a refreshing wellspring to the visitor. There are great exhibitions and there will be more. But when you find these jewels of display and interpretation, you generally will find they are the result of one or two very gifted people—people who have imagination and taste —qualities that you cannot buy in capsules at your corner drugstore. We are only limited by ourselves, and the results of our work will reflect our taste and knowledge.

New exhibitions are really old exhibitions to the degree that the objects are the same. New exhibitions are the result of people rearranging objects in new contexts. A new exhibition or interpretation is the result of imagination and taste. A great exhibition is not the result of a group endeavor but the reflection of an individual.

Museum Interpretation of Western History

Museum Philosophy and Practice

Merrill J. Mattes

What is a history museum? It can be a lot of things, ranging from the cluttered assortment of sea shells and German war helmets in the Podunk County Courthouse basement to the vast marbled corridors and warehouse displays of "everything under the sun" in Washington's old U. S. National. A museum can also be a place with a single distinctive and compelling theme, revealed by live, colorful exhibits which blend objects and illustrations and words into a meaningful and exciting whole. This is what a National Park Service museum tries to be. In its broader sense, a museum can also be a historic structure restoration, where the past is recreated on a life-size scale, rather than in miniature or in fragments.

The word "museum" still conjures up the musty aroma of Indian burials and Egyptian mummies. For many years it had an understandably depressing effect on Congressional committees, so more recently an effort has been made to play down "museums" and stress "exhibit rooms," "interpretive displays," and "visitor centers." Evidently this fresh terminology has helped, because National Park Service museums are today enjoying an unprecedented revival. The number of our historical areas west of the Mississippi River, once negligible in contrast to the East, is growing in the favorable climate of economic prosperity and the dynamic leadership of Director Conrad L. Wirth and Secretary Stewart L. Udall. These museums (often in handsome new visitor centers) become repositories of knowledge for scholar and layman alike. National Park Service museums are both sources and interpreters of history, on a more popular comprehension level than libraries or archives, perhaps, but no less vital to the appreciation of Western America.

It has been stated recently that the interstate highway cloverleaf is becoming our national flower, and this is a sobering thought because the wide western landscape, with its expanse of sage-brush, distant mountain peaks, and blue horizon, is now being conquered by concrete—not only highways but galloping city suburbs, airports, parking lots, Atlas launching pads, and A & W root-beer drive-ins. As our primeval landscape is threatened, something is happening also to our traditions, our cultural values. We may not be able to roll back the concrete, but we can do something about the values. We can preserve authentic historic sites and structures which remind us of ancestral virtues and triumphs, and we can interpret these to a culturally thirsty public. That's what historic museums and restorations are for.

Five principles of museum philosophy and practice occur to me. There are doubtless others, or these can probably be boiled down into one underlying principle, but let me suggest five which cannot be ignored if a museum is to succeed:

1. *Integrity of Theme:* If there is a vital story to tell, define the story, and then stick to it. Avoid drifting into irrelevancies and generalities. A museum that is nationally significant should reinforce and enrich the visitors' impression of a single great moment, or a great movement, or a great place or personality in American history.

2. *Uncompromising Research:* Nothing is taken for granted. No interpretation, however time-honored, is too sacred to withstand the continuing searching scrutiny of all discoverable sources. This "Fearless Fosdick" approach to research does not always have happy results. One of our areas, Verendrye National Monument in North Dakota, had to be abolished when a tenacious researcher demonstrated that the French explorer could not have come within 50 miles of said monument!

3. *Respect for the Historic Object:* The original idea of a museum was to display objects. But there has been a modern temptation to "tell a story," sometimes with such a passion for artwork and labored verbosity that the object itself gets shoved into the background or, in some instances, is omitted altogether. We aim to restore the historic object (including the historic building) to its rightful central place. History museums should preserve and illu-

minate history, and not attempt to be a showcase for modern artists and label-writers.

4. *Artistic Balance:* Veneration for the object does not eliminate the artist; rather, it places a premium on the artistic ingenuity of the museum designer and curator, to arrange things in such a way as to bring the theme into brilliant focus, to give the object a halo of excitement, and to make the old historic building once again alive with a vision of ancient glory. In a history museum, bad art distorts history; good art serves to put history in a fresh and glowing perspective.

5. *Respect for the Visitor:* Perhaps I should say, respect for the intelligence and the comfort of the visitor. Unlike certain modern art museums which are for artists, history museums are for people. There are all kinds of people, but there is a tendency among us to under-rate their average IQ and educational background, and to over-rate their endurance. Spaciousness of structural design, the graceful flow of the story line, lighting vivid yet unobstrusive, benches to ease weary bones, all of these things are designed into an effective museum or restoration. If the visitor is jostled, confused, blinded, and fatigued, he will scarcely get that inspirational message which is the only excuse for an historic shrine being supported by the taxpayers in the first place.

I suggest two good examples of new historical museums which fulfill these five principles—Homestead, near Beatrice, Nebraska, and Theodore Roosevelt National Memorial Park, at Medora, North Dakota.

In 1938 Daniel Freeman's 160-acre farm, long advertised, with some poetic license, as "the First Homestead," became by Congressional courtesy the Homestead National Monument. For over twenty years the area languished, and the scarce or accidental visitor had to find what inspiration he could in gazing out over Freeman's rather ordinary quarter-section. Things improved somewhat when we were able to move in and restore the remains of the old, tipsy, but bona fide log dwelling of George Washington Palmer, a neighboring homesteader of 1867. But the great day did not arrive until 1962 when, during the Centennial Year of President Lincoln's signature on the Homestead Act, we were able to complete and dedicate a museum which is a worthy reminder of a democratic movement which helped to populate the Great Plains.

Here, on the banks of Cub Creek, within view of restored blue-stem meadows as well as endless Nebraska cornfields, is a museum which captures the essence of homesteading both as economic impact and as personal experience. A wealth of primitive agrarian and domestic implements are interwoven with blow-ups of rare photographs and bright settings to create a mood of kinship with the weather-beaten folks who got on with the unglamorous job of settling the West. Of particular impact are a "sod-busting" diorama and a giant mural of a tiny prairie home in a vast sweep of storm-threatened prairie,—both overpowering the beholder with a sense of the homesteaders' elemental struggle for survival.

The saga of Teddy Roosevelt in the Little Missouri Badlands can be flavored in a tour of the Memorial Park, and particularly in a pilgrimage by jeep to the remote Elkhorn Ranch site. But this bit of rugged Americana can best be understood by a visit to the old cattle town of Medora. Here—in private or state ownership—are buildings such as the Rough Rider's Hotel, the Ferris Store, and the Chateau de Mores, all Roosevelt contemporaries. And here also at the Memorial Park headquarters, the National Park Service has built a museum which brings Teddy back to life. There is a diorama re-creating the Elkhorn Ranch, scenes of adventure and disaster in the early range cattle industry, cattle brands, cowboy paraphernalia, and biographical highlights of the New York dude who fell in love with the desolate badlands. A fine collection of Roosevelt gear and the liberal application of his pithy quotations, along with a small dose of Badlands geology, flora and fauna, make this museum a live one. An outdoor exhibit, within a few steps of the lobby, is the fully restored Maltese Cross cabin, now in its final resting place after early dismemberment and journeys to several World Fairs.

All good museums are not necessarily new; but old museums do become antiquated in style (this may be the fate of our new museums twenty years from now); so sometimes, like the family jalopy, they are overhauled. Good examples of rejuvenation are to be found at Scotts Bluff and Custer Battlefield National Monuments.

Scotts Bluff, a majestic landmark on the old Oregon Trail, would make a fine monument all by itself, but our recently renovated Old Oregon Trail Museum does help to make more vivid and meaningful the experience of the covered wagon emigrant. The 1936 version of this museum was really an unabashed art gallery of the trans-

Mississippi West, a series of well-documented WPA paintings, with the only objects those scrounged by the custodian and scattered around without any particular logic. In 1940 a paleontology wing was added, to display fossils of the neighborhood (violation of Rule One, Integrity of Theme). In 1943 the William H. Jackson Memorial Room was added, featuring sketches made by the artist in 1866 as a bullwhacker on the Trail. But it was not until 1962 that we set things to rights with a new Landmark Room (the story of Scotts Bluff itself, and its earliest visitors) and a new Oregon Trail Room (the story of the migrations). Everything extraneous we shipped elsewhere; now we have a museum that has both vitality and integrity, emphasizing the dramatic role of Scotts Bluff in the great migrations up the Platte River Road.

Custer Battlefield was the first western area to get a museum after World War II, a museum dedicated to the tragic affair of 1876, wrapped around the George Armstrong Custer Collection, bequeathed by that Number One Custer fan, Mrs. George Armstrong Custer (who survived her illustrious spouse by some 60 years). Dedication of this museum occurred in 1951. It has taken twelve long years of research and historical perspective to appreciate the defects of this first effort—inaccuracies in data and use of objects, hiatuses, superfluities, and imbalance in the treatment of component parts. So we are now in the throes of a drastic revision of the museum at Custer Battlefield in which we are striving for more accuracy (thanks in part to a mine detector survey of Custer's route and the Reno-Benteen siege area), more emphasis on the enlisted man who did most of the dying, and more elbow room for the nearly 200,000 people who swarm over the premises each summer.

We also have "special situation" museums, that is, ones that are unique and inimitable. In this category, I place Grand Teton, Mount Rushmore, and Jefferson National Expansion Memorial.

Grand Teton is the only major National Park, to my knowledge, that has a first-class *historical* museum, with the usual assortment of rocks, flora, and fauna displayed elsewhere. This is the Fur Trade Museum in the visitor center at Park headquarters, Jackson Hole, Wyoming. Here is an unabashed effort to tell the near-legendary but authenticated story of Rocky Mountain fur trade and exploration. It is to the eternal credit of National Park Service administrators that they went along with the idea of breaching the traditional barrier beween scenic National Park and unscenic historic monument and, in 1960, dedicated an *historic* museum in a *scenic* National Park.

The Fur Trade Museum, enticing over 1200 visitors daily, is a rare blend of scenes, maps, and historic objects illustrating the Homeric saga of Colter, Bridger, Sublette, Fitzpatrick, and other fur trade immortals who haunted those parts, with a staccato accompaniment of flintlock and percussion firearms, traps, accessories, and trade goods in sufficient array to bedazzle the most ardent antiquarian. In no other museum is history, geography, and artistry more skillfully blended.

At Mount Rushmore are the busts of four great Presidents sculptured out of a mountain-top, granite heroes on a colossal scale. Millions of tourists gravitate to Rushmore and are awe-struck by the grandeur of the sculpture and its sheer physical proportions. So why bother with a museum?

Well, at first we thought we should improve on Gutzon Borglum, the sculptor, and develop a museum that would explain the patriotic symbolism. But the more we tried to define the symbolism in museum terms, the more difficult became our task. We came to realize that great sculpture, like great poetry, cannot be captured and reduced to a manageable series of concepts. And we came to realize further that the Great American Tourist came to Rushmore as a temple, like the Lincoln Memorial in Washington, D. C., to be spiritually refreshed. We came to realize, in short, that no museum was needed to reinforce the patriotic impact.

There *will* be a small secondary museum to tell of Borglum and the men behind the idea of the Memorial, and of the methods of construction, with dynamite and jackhammer, but no museum of the four Presidents. Our new visitor center has only a vast view terrace, and four immortal quotations emblazoned by the sun.

Another unusual example, and surely the one least likely to be imitated, is that of Jefferson National Expansion Memorial, on the site of the early village of St. Louis. This is an area of 80 acres on the Mississippi River waterfront, adjoining downtown St. Louis, which will be graced by one of the great architectural monuments of the twentieth century, a slender stainless steel arch 630 feet high —the Gateway Memorial Arch designed by the late Eero Saarinen— complete with elevators. At the base of this incredible structure will be an underground visitor center with a museum of mammoth proportions, some 40,000 square feet, or the equivalent of one football field, which will be devoted to twelve major chapters of territorial expansion west of the Mississippi. In this context, obviously, ordinary museum methods will not serve; endless rows of the normal combinations of pictures, maps, labels, and artifacts would induce sleep-walking or screaming hysteria. Although there are museums and art galleries on this scale elsewhere, there is none other with such singleness of theme. Here, indeed, is a premium upon ingenuity, and we think—we hope—that this challenge has been met with a variety of new devices. These include labyrinthine corridors with frequent "escape hatches" for those given to claustrophobia; paintings and photomurals of heroic proportions; life-size diorama sequences; statuary; and a generous array of historical materials gathered from sixteen Western states. A documentary movie, shown in twin theatres, will set the mood for this museum

It is probably a bit of an anticlimax to confess that no money is adventure.
available within present Congressional limitations to complete the planned exhibits for this museum of epic proportions. Almost all of our project assets—some $12,000,000—are now going into the Gargantuan Arch; indeed, at this moment, the Arch is under construction, its triangular bowlegs beginning to creep skyward. However, visitors to our "open house" in 1964—the Bicentennial of St. Louis—will have *some* exposure to history. In the lobby there will be twelve exhibits, samples of the ultimate twelve units, and one theatre to show the documentary movie of the historic West.

No discussion of what's new in the western half of the National Park System would be complete without a word on historical restorations. Among minor projects is the aforementioned Maltese Cross Cabin at Theodore Roosevelt headquarters, which had to be trundled down the highway 150 miles from Bismarck, fitted out with an appropriate roof, and refurnished on the basis of research rather than the D.A.R. sentiment that invested the Bismarck version.

Two restorations fascinate visitors to Jackson Hole. One is the lonely Cunningham Cabin, where alleged horse-thieves were gunned down by an alleged posse, way back about 1890. The other is Menor's Ferry, with crude log buildings and a working cable ferryboat over Snake River, as actually used during the 1920's (that's medieval time in Jackson Hole) by settlers who never dreamed that they were living in what was about to become one of the world's most spectacular mountain parks.

Other scenic National Parks are developing an interest in their history. The most active in this field is Yosemite National Park in California where, near the covered bridge and Old Inn at Mariposa Big Grove, the park naturalist has assembled a fine collection of old Wells Fargo stage stations, ranger stations, prospectors' shacks, etc., from the far corners of the park. A more modest effort, still in the planning stage, is the restoration of the Old Soldier Station at Norris Junction, Yellowstone Park, solitary relic of the early days, when the U. S. Army patrolled the geyser basins.

Of course, no restoration tingles the blood quite so much as an old fort—military or trading post. In fact, these have such an appeal to a generation nurtured on television horse operas that the countryside is becoming infested with fake replicas. The real authentic article is harder to find.

We are thinking about the full-scale restoration of three famous trading posts. These are Bent's Old Fort near La Junta, Colorado, which was a massive adobe structure on the Santa Fe Trail; the Grand Portage, Minnesota, post of the British Northwest Company of 1790; and the Fort Union trading post of the American Fur Company on the North Dakota-Montana boundary, capitol of the Upper Missouri fur trade. (The first two are established National Park units; Fort Union—not to be confused with the military depot of the same name in New Mexico—is a proposal now before Congress.)

The hypothetical restoration of Fort Clatsop, the Lewis and Clark wintering place near Astoria, Oregon, was undertaken before we took over the place. This, like Fort Osage in Jackson County, Missouri (a Registered National Historic Landmark), and the three above mentioned, is in the category of entire reconstruction, or restoration from scratch, so to speak, where random travelers' notes and meagre archeological evidence are the only original remains.

Genuine restoration as such, where a somehow surviving structure or group of structures is put back into pristine condition, applies conspicuously at two military posts, which loomed large in the pacification of the Great Plains: Fort Davis in West Texas, and Fort Laramie on the Oregon-California Trail, in eastern Wyoming. The contrasting treatment of these two restorations proves in another way that the National Park Service is not in a bureaucratic rut, with one straitjacket solution for everything.

The remains we inherited at Fort Davis are extensive, but largely in the form of roofless ruins. The planned solution here is restoration of this military post to its total *appearance* at the time of its climactic development in the 1880's. Three buildings—barracks, commanding officer's quarters, and hospital—will be completely restored and refurnished. A fourth, another barracks, will be restored only to its external appearance and used as a museum. On the remaining ruins, authentic roofs and porches will be superimposed, on independent supports, and the illusion, at least, of Fort Davis in its heyday will be complete.

When serious restoration work began at Fort Laramie in 1950—sixty years after abandonment—the remains consisted of about ten standing ruins, and a similar number of major structures still roughly intact, but all on the verge of collapse. The formula here, which was evolved with much soul-searching and debate over the next decade, was not restoration of the entire fort to any given period but, rather, preservation of the picturesque ruins, and restoration of each intact structure to its individual period of maximum importance. Since the military history of Fort Laramie extended from 1849 to 1890, this makes quite a spread in time scale. The adobe trading post section of the Sutler's Store and the handsome two-storied quarters called Old Bedlam go back to the California Gold Rush. Various officers' quarters represent the decades of the 1870's and 1880's. By this "outdoor museum" approach, we are also able to exhibit all of the three successive guardhouses: the grim masonry block of 1866, the concrete version of 1876, and (recently discovered underneath the latter) the remains of the solitary confinement cells of 1850. Fort Laramie as restored today admittedly resembles no single period of its history. The complete evolution of the physical fort, and its role in the pageant of the West, will be presented to the visitor before his parade ground tour by exhibits in a new and separate visitor center.

Structural restoration is being undertaken, of course, with Federal funds, at an estimated completion cost of over $300,000; but it should be noted that a blow for private enterprise has been struck by Mrs. Charles S. Hill of Denver, Colorado, who is very generously underwriting the cost—some $100,000—of interior furnishings for the restored buildings. If the visitor center and other new de-

velopment features cost what we expect them to, the total Fort
Laramie restoration will have a price tag of around $1,000,000.

Good museums and good restorations cost money, that is true;
but in terms of pride in our American heritage, this represents a
priceless investment in the future.

Problems of Western Museums

James T. Forrest

The interpretation of history by our museums is essential to their
growing role as educational institutions. In the pursuit of this relatively new role the state and local historical agencies in the West
have encountered certain unique problems. These stem, in part,
from the autonomous and individualistic nature of the agencies
themselves. Unlike, for example, the National Park Service—which
by its very nature is able to employ its specialists effectively across
the board, assist the lowest levels, and maintain an even presentation standard—the western state and local historical agencies are
characterized by an extreme diversity of capability, funds, talent,
and physical facilities. In some ways, this is good; in others, perhaps not so. However, it is a situation that must be frankly
recognized.

Certainly, active local effort and diversity conform to certain of
our democratic concepts. Any sort of centralization or autonomous
control of the museums of western state and local historical agencies
would be manifestly impossible and even undesirable.

However, a greater exchange of ideas is highly desirable between
the western museums—the kind of exchange that was made possible by this joint session. After all, these museums have, to a great
extent, common goals and problems. Furthermore, as became
clearly apparent during a recent exchange of correspondence that
I had with the various directors on this very subject, they are
anxious to talk about their problems, to make recommendations, to
learn from others, and, all in all, to insure an enhanced capability
in telling the story of western history accurately and effectively.
There is a healthy spirit in the air.

Indeed, there is a healthy spirit among the western state and local historical museum agencies in many respects. They have a freshness, vigor, and robustness that is characteristic of the West itself. They are, by and large, newer than those in the East and have had a chance to get a fresh start. They have young and eager personnel. They have probably had less shifting of personnel than many eastern institutions. They are receptive to new ideas and approaches, and probably are more prone to experiment. Certainly excellent progress has been made by the western museums in the presentation of history.

The western museums, too, as a whole, have a series of unique problems—many of which, again, are inherent on the western scene: the problem of attendance because of sparse settlement; the spasmodic nature of attendance because of the summer tourist influx; more "competition" from commercial museums; inadequate supporting services, such as printing facilities; an isolation and poor communication with the profession; meagre financial and physical resources; and, finally, because they are new, a lack of experience. Their special technical problem is to show the unique contribution of the West to American development and why the West developed differently from the Middle West and East.

Yet, despite the existence of these comparatively unique problems, the western museums are strongly affected by national currents in the field. Most of their basic problems are shared with their counterparts in the East; both the eastern and western agencies have a common denominator of motivation and intent. The motivation and intent are quite obvious, and so need not detain us here. The problems are another matter.

The problems facing the western museums—many of which are shared with those in the East—can be broken down into three distinct areas: presentation philosophy, communications, and public relations.

The matter of presentation philosophy has been swirling around our heads since Colonial days and will probably continue to do so as the first museums are established on the moon or Mars. Even though it is a subject that sometimes when broached results in fist fights, it is nevertheless one that gets to the very heart of the matter and does not resolve itself by being shunted aside. Fortunately, there is a growing concern on the part of museum people as to the effectiveness of current presentation methods.

All of us are familiar with the general trend of presentation philosophy through the years. The crowded, gloomy, shelf-and-case cluttered museum of yesterday has given way to the airy, light, spacious, interpretive museum of today. Mass has given way to singularity. Curios have given way to didacticism. Certainly no one denies that a great improvement has been made. However, I have felt for some time that the pendulum has swung too far and that a better balance needs to be achieved between the old and the new. I now find that I am not alone in this thinking.

Much of the change can be traced to the ascendancy of the designer—God bless him, whom we know was sorely needed. Yet perhaps he has ascended a bit too far—especially in relation to the core of the matter: the *presentation* of history. Isn't a better liaison between designer and curator clearly in order? Isn't the designer's "clean sweep" often *too* clean and lacking in historical substance? And, in this sense, haven't we moved too much away from our central goal into the realm of the "pretty", the eye-catching and the spectacular—which run parallel to the public relations devices used by some institutions: the hoopla, the dancing girls, gala openings, and the like. The swing has been so far that story and exhibit often suffer from a paucity of specimens, and even these are sometimes lost in poor choice of background and accent colors or oversize cut-out letters. A tendency toward sameness in exhibits is evident across the country. Regional "flavor" and institutional individuality are fading. As a result, we have a kind of sterility.

What is clearly needed is better cooperation between designer and curator—a cooperation that needs to be worked out on the local level—to insure more substantive exhibits. "Looks" must be better blended with substance.

When this is done, we will see an end to the "billboard" type of exhibit which is common today. By "billboard" I mean the ultra-interpretive type of exhibit which uses few artifacts and often has the general design and appearance of a billboard—but which makes only one major point and which is often almost free of textual matter. This is in contrast to the old method of showing a lot, telling a lot, but leaving the interpretation to the viewer.

The trouble with the "billboard" approach is that it assumes that the museum visitor will be there only a short time, is perhaps not very interested in the subject to begin with, and that he must be enticed and entertained visually—in the interest of education. He must be whacked over the head, so to speak.

There seems to be evidence that this basic assumption is wrong; or, at least in our interest in hitting the mass of the people, we are not only failing to realize the full potentiality of our audience but are also being unfair to part of it. In other words, our audience is broader and has greater depth than we realize. Certainly, it seems desirable to swing the pendulum a bit, to blend the old and the new. Here are some straws in the wind.

Miss Lola Homsher, Director of the Wyoming State Archives and Historical Department, presents the problem very aptly:

"'Our museum is what Mari Sandoz referred to as a research museum and one she was pleased to study. I have learned through the comments of our visitors that they are delighted to see one museum where they can look at objects, read our descriptive cards, and do some interpretation of their own. There is so much of the billboard type of display that people find ours refreshing.

"Very frankly I would like to combine the billboard type of display. I do know that because of our visitors' comments I do not want to go into the interpretive displays entirely."

Mr. H. J. Swinney, Director of the Idaho Historical Society, also has some qualms:

"I am committed to the interpretive method of display, although I must admit that I continue to have twinges of doubt about it. I confess that, not uncommonly, we find our public giving minimal attention to interpretive displays which we have spent a lot of time on, and then peering for a long time into the few old-fashioned 'hodge-podge' cases which still remain in some of our corners. I rationalize this by assuming either that the idea of our interpretive displays gets over very quickly, or else the individual I have watched is not very much interested in the particular subject of the interpretive display. I go a step further by thinking that a lot of time is spent in front of the old-fashioned cases because they are so hard to see into and understand. But I still can't be absolutely certain that all of our present interpretive work is right.

"As the pendulum of exhibit style has swung away from the crowded cases of half a century ago toward the highly didactic designs of today, I think it may have swung past the reasonable center point. Where we used to have all objects and no labels (so to speak) we are now getting to the point where we have all labels and no objects. I think that most museum people instinctively believe in the exhibition of objects, and that we will therefore see a swing of the pendulum back toward more and more objects in cases."

Mr. Carroll D. Hall, Monument Supervisor at Sutter's Fort, a state historical monument, Sacramento, California, provides us with some other evidence. He states that some years ago when the Fort was converted from a museum of the California period (1839-1860) to a restoration, in which process the old exhibit cases were removed, the public response was not one of "undiluted hallelujahs." Those who remembered the artifacts complain that there is now "nothing to see." For these reasons, the present master plan, in some instances, involves a full circle, and includes plans to restore some exhibits which had been removed.

Mr. Hall says: "We hear much of modern techniques, audio-visual this and that, spatial concepts, and visitor-flow, when all the visitor wants to see is something he recognizes. The colorful, billboard type of display . . . with few artifacts . . . often is sterile."

Mr. Marvin Kivett, Director of the Nebraska State Historical Society, informs me that, because his institution recognizes that collections of items have interest, they have set up a "Collector's Lane", in which large collections of glassware, guns, arrowheads, and other groups of items are exhibited. His institution also employs a series of full-scale period rooms. It also uses dioramas as interpretive aids rather than as ends in themselves. Mr. Kivett says that public response is good.

Mr. Russell E. Belous, Associate Curator, Western History, Los Angeles County Museum, states that "Where there has been public criticism of the new approach in design, it is because of the lack of original objects. . . ." Mr. William E. Marshall, Executive Director of the State Historical Society of Colorado, feels that "many new 'gimmicks' do not in fact do the job intended."

Not that there is any clear-cut right or wrong between the old and new methods of exhibition, nor any conclusive evidence as to which is the most effective; unfortunately, few studies have been made, although the Milwaukee Public Museum is now making a study in depth. In a sense the question is academic. It is a matter of how best to do the job. It seems quite apparent, however, that we should allow more room for special exhibits and comprehensive collections—which do not necessarily have to be related to a "story" and which encourage collectors and specialists. This is not to say that we should not interpret; however, some interpretation should be left to the viewer.

A workable resolution of the interpretive-object clash, and the determination of just how far the pendulum should be regulated, can be resolved only by considering a very fundamental point: the bases for a museum's existence. Certainly, one of the important ones is to teach—to instruct—by displaying physical objects. We *exhibit* objects to *teach,* not to *entertain.* If this were not true, it would be more of an art gallery than a museum—which is central to the point I am trying to make. And, indeed, with the ascendancy of designers, they have—inadvertently or not—taken a step in the direction of turning our museums into art-entertainment galleries.

Granted, of course, that the public has a right to expect modern design and lighting techniques, and the effective use of the latest visual and audio devices. Clearly, the art of communication has become more sophisticated, and we are all happy to live with it. The selective, interpretive type of exhibit is here to stay. It is as much with us as jet aircraft.

But, as teachers, we must teach well. We cannot expect the public to dig deeply to extract information from our exhibits; but rather that the educational process be a pleasant one. Here is where the designer can play a vital role, *but* working in close coordination with the curator. The objects must not be de-emphasized or shunted aside. Clearly a good exhibit must contain enough material to tell the story—but with more rather than fewer objects if there is any question. After all, a museum is functioning best when it provides the visitor with a rewarding "visual experience."

In the final analysis, it is the museum director who must determine what balance to strike between the esthetic propensities of the designer and the factual knowledge and technical know-how of the curator. Certainly, the total interpretive-object balance in museums today needs to be carefully re-examined

Enough for the matter of presentation philosophy. Now to turn to another important problem area: communications. *All* museums, not only those in the West, have a long way to go in the broad area because it runs the gamut from communicating in exhibits themselves to the broader areas of communication with the public. Let's look at communication in the museum itself, in exhibits. Here we still face some staggering problems. Take the matter of labeling, for example, one that is perhaps mundane and not too dramatic—but vitally important. Certainly it is illustrative of the basic communications problems we are facing.

Some of the problems in labeling are general and some specific. From a general standpoint, just how much labeling is needed? As in the case of presentation philosophy, there is much evidence that in labeling the pendulum has swung too far toward the cryptic and the telegraphic. A better balance needs be struck. More adequate labeling is needed. Here again we face the ascendancy of the designer. Many of the modern interpretive exhibits are not properly labeled, apparently because labels would interfere with esthetics. The tendency seems to be toward shorter labels, even in didactic exhibits. This is carried to the point that little information, if any, is imparted. Is there any reason why every object in a case should not, or cannot, be labeled or properly identified? To take the approach that any label but the most telegraphic will bore the visitors is to deprive many of them of their privilege and right to glean information in depth. A good general rule for all labels is: follow the journalistic rule of Who, What, Where, When, and sometimes Why. Maps, diagrams, drawings, often help in combination with words to get these essential facts to the interested viewer. (The important identification material should come first on the label; the development of the "headline" may even follow in smaller type.)

Because museum visitors *do* read, label copy should be reasonably comprehensive. *And,* to turn to the specific problem in labeling, above all they should be *well-written*. A basic problem in labeling today—and probably yesterday too— is plain old clarity, vocabulary level, grammar, and syntax. And, sometimes, common sense.

When an exhibit is collated especially for school children, vocabulary levels should be checked with educational authorities; that is, at least when the person writing the label is not aware of a simple truth—the simple word is most often the best. And, certainly, in view of all the studies that have been made of vocabulary level of the general populace, good *general* rules for adults and children are: simple words, short sentences, direct statements, and the elimination of ambiguities. Editorial personnel should certainly be utilized if they are available. It is an area that must be given constant attention.

Another problem in communications with the public is in a broader area than the exhibits themselves. A museum today must be more than a place for exhibits. The public now expects research and study collections as well, an area in which many museums do not have balanced programs. Most important of all, the results of research and the extent of museum activities must be communicated to the public. This can be done effectively through publications and educational programs.

Publications have the special advantage of providing a degree of public relations permanence. They can serve as "little ambassadors" abroad in the land for the museum involved. Furthermore, often they are rather easily obtainable byproducts of exhibitions and represent a salvaging for the permanent record of the great amount of effort that goes into the preparation of the exhibit which would otherwise be lost. The transiency of major exhibits is not only unfortunate but frequently represents a loss of historical information once the exhibit is dismantled and dispersed.

With the proper planning early in the preparations for an exhibit, it is somewhat surprising how easily the research and effort that are involved can be coordinated with an ultimate publication. This is a method that has proved to be highly effective for us at the Museum of New Mexico. Our editor is involved in a liaison capacity in exhibit planning from the very beginning. Once labels are prepared, he edits them with final publication aspects in mind. The twofold advantage is that we not only get a publication but we get better labels—something that is obviously highly desirable.

Hence, before the exhibition is even opened to the public we have a good publication for the permanent record on the press. We have found that these publications sell very well at exhibit time, greatly enhancing the Museum's communications and, incidentally, being of some help from a budget standpoint.

A second important phase in communications is an educational program. Certainly, not all museums can have a full-fledged educational program, but the function should always be kept in the foreground. Sometimes, a part-time person can be assigned this duty. In any event, it is rather amazing what an effective tool a good educational program can be—not only for the school children but also for the museum. It has the advantage of offering valuable communication with some key citizens, teachers, and parents. Certainly, a museum can serve a vital role in the interpretation of state or regional history—and in the West this is often a factor, since state history text books at the grade school level are not always adequate for modern teaching methods. We have found that close liaison with the state educational authorities is not only desirable but necessary. Our state museum must be prepared to fill in some wide gaps in the state history curriculum. Frequently, school children visiting our museum receive their first introduction to the state's long and colorful past.

There is no doubt in our minds that effective publications and educational programs are powerful communications tools.

The third problem area that I would like to touch on involves public relations. This is a broad subject, of course, but I would like to mention only one specific area of the subject. That is, that public relations programs should always be in keeping with the museum's intended image. There has been a somewhat disconcerting tendency recently on the part of some museums to lean a little too far toward the commercial "sell-the-product" approach. This is not to advocate, of course, a return to cloistered academe or a stuffy aloofness. It is to advocate a closer look at any public relations program to insure the proper balance. Public relations zest and dignity are not incompatible. In this age of commercialization we must be aware of the dangers of following the seemingly lucrative trail to "Old Pioneer Land"—with its misinterpretation and nonsensical treatment of the history of our people and our land.

From my knowledge of what museums in the West are doing and from the reports I have gotten, from Montana to California to Nebraska, it would appear that the museum professionals are very aware of their task. They recognize that the problem is one of communication—that they must approach the matter as historians, educators, designers, and curators. One museum learns from another and museums do learn from organizations with similar problems or needs. The West does not have distinct or unique requirements for its presentation and interpretation of history, but it may approach the solution with some advantages and some disadvantages. The museums, by and large, seem responsive to their purpose and recognize that *no other institution in the community can or will do the job if they do not.* Theirs is a vital contribution to the cultural resources of their respective areas. The color and the drama of the western movement may lend the museum personnel some opportunities not common in other regions; this greatest of modern migrations may provide a running theme for their story. Materials may be more readily available in these more recently settled states—but the problems of communication and interpretation, alas, remain pretty much the same for all parts of the country.

The western museums are doing well, in my opinion. Perhaps better communication between museums would help. Very likely, museum directors could learn from non-museum educators about students and what they respond best to—but museums are now fully aware of their role and they are steadily moving towards more effective use of the talent, the materials, and the improved facilities at their disposal. And the public is flocking to our museums —they like what they see.

Comments

John W. Jenkins

Although I might nit-pick and disagree with some statements in each of the papers presented by Merrill Mattes and Jim Forrest, I prefer to extend their remarks by admitting that their complaints about lack of cooperation by exhibits designers are somewhat justified. For several years I have been a non-historian laboring among historians—a kind of mediator between historians on the one side and designers and artists on the other.

So it was with no great shock that I read Merrill's and Jim's statements of dissatisfaction with exhibits in which the designer had somehow gained ascendency over the historian. In general, I believe such instances are due to lack of communication and the conceits of the two individuals concerned. I also believe that more historians are learning to get along with designers, just as they have learned to get along with editors. In other words, just as they have learned to accept some of the idiosyncracies of editorial dictums in relation to the printing and publishing of their writings, some historians have also learned to meet the requests and demands of designers who are sincerely attempting to create a visual presentation of a narrative approach to some aspect of history.

In defense of the historians, I would be quick to reprimand the designer who ignores or uses specimens poorly or obscurely in exhibits. However, in defense of the designer, there are too few historians who are knowledgeable of the visual materials—such as the contemporary maps, sketches, paintings, photographs, and cultural objects which relate closely or specifically to their subject. Because of this lack of knowledge, the designer often must resort to designing a non-objective, yet visual, exhibit to carry an essential but wholly verbal portion of the story which the historian insists is necessary in the exhibits.

Fortunately, there is a growing, but still too small, number of historians, most of them in history museums and major restorations, who are devoting their studies to historic objects as well as to documentary sources. Admittedly this is a difficult and frustrating field of research because many of these cultural objects are widely scattered across the country, hidden in poorly cataloged collections in museums or in collectors' homes, in second-hand and antique stores, and even in junk piles at times. For many years history museums have had to rely on collectors and hobbyists for information and identification of much of the material in the museum collections. These collectors, bless them, have succeeded in accumulating vast quantities of historic objects and through various publications, sponsored and published by collectors' associations, have begun to give us, through a respectable level and type of research, much information about these historic materials.

Museum workers also owe thanks to non-historians such as the late Robert Taft, a chemistry professor, who became interested enough in tracing collections to produce two very useful books on the early artists, illustrators, and photographers of the West. Another such man is Carl Russell, a naturalist by training and for some years chief of the National Park Service's interpretation program, who became a student of the objects of the fur trade. He has not been successful in obtaining publication of much of his extensive and accumulated information on the fur trade, but the University of California Press did publish his *Guns of the Early Frontiers* (Berkeley, 1957).

I think we must admit that the art and science museums, including those in which ethnological materials have found space, are far ahead of history museums in scholarly research and knowledge of the objects in their collections. I believe that if we are to improve our history museums, there must be a renewal of efforts by museums and universities to attract well-trained historians into well-planned, museum-oriented research projects. Then history museums can fulfill the threefold functions of all good museums: to collect and preserve, to study, and to interpret their collections.

I am sorry to see doubts in the minds of so many historical society directors toward "interpretive" displays or exhibits. I believe such pronouncements are akin to the statement, "Perhaps we should stop publishing books." We cannot afford to slip backwards almost 70 years to before the time when George Brown Goode stated that a good museum exhibit should be a well written story illustrated by carefully selected specimens, but we can supplement interpretive exhibits by installing "collectors lanes" or study-exhibition collections. However, the specimens in such exhibits should also be interpreted for the uninitiated visitors to broaden their scope of understanding. But please, rather than giving up on interpretive exhibits, let us try to improve them to make them more meaningful and interesting for the visitors.

Though exhibits are my "business" I admit freely that they are not an end in themselves nor always the best means of interpretation. So long as we can obtain and use carefully selected and intelligently and tastefully presented specimens, exhibits have certain advantages over other methods of presentation, and I believe many history museums have succeeded in improving their exhibits presentation. However, history museums often lag behind the efforts and techniques of art and science museums in the presentation of illustrated lectures, programs of various types, gallery tours for adults (as well as school groups), movies, and in the production of exhibition catalogs and well written, edited, and illustrated publications. All of these can supplement, complement, and expand the understanding of what can be seen in the exhibits.

I hope you do not think this was my attempt to sneak in a third paper—it has been intended as a type of defense against some of Merrill's, Jim's, and others' unkind remarks about "sterile, too colorful, billboard-type displays, and other gadgetry" which have crept into museum exhibits. The good exhibit techniques will stay and be improved upon, but much of what we dislike now will pass on into limbo as other items of bad taste have passed on, out of sight and memory.

Dollars and Cents and Historic Sites

Clifford L. Lord

Historic sites cost money. Initial capital requirements are always substantial, for authenticity in restoration or reconstruction is never cheap—though obviously the frontier sod-house or log cabin is not as costly as the stage-coach tavern, which in turn is of a different magnitude of cost than a Colonial Williamsburg. But initial outlay which just introduces the problem, is usually taken care of through foundation support, other private philanthropy, or government expenditure. Then starts the year-in and year-out struggle to meet the costs of maintenance and operation.

Maintenance involves keeping the building (or buildings) and contents clean and tidy, in good repair and insured, and seeing that the grounds are well kept. It also entails the long-range costs of depreciation—roofs, foundations, and all that lies between. Operation involves the care (and often feeding) of the visitor: collecting admissions, policing the properties, and—of prime importance—educating the guest by initial oral presentation, introductory film, guide service, taped recordings at various stages of the tour, or pageantry—including the recently introduced *son et lumière*—, singly or in tandem. An oral presentation must be carried off with accuracy and flair. A film, unless very well done, will be a fiasco. Guides must be well-trained, courteous, sufficiently knowledgeable to discuss the site intelligently, correctly, and helpfully with the great variety of visitors who will ask a great variety of questions from a great variety of backgrounds. Costumes—regularly cleaned and pressed—add color and a sense of authenticity. Pageantry must be well done if done at all. And all—together with the administrative staff which grows as the number of activities and functions grow—cost money.

Money comes to a site from many sources. Federally-owned sites are supported almost entirely by the taxpayer. The financing of state-owned sites varies greatly from state to state. Wisconsin has successfully insisted from the outset that its state-owned sites must be substantially self-supporting, that their costs must be borne primarily by those who benefit from visiting the sites rather than by the general taxpayer. At the other pole is the state which, like the federal government, offers almost total tax support. In between lie many others.

Municipalities most often offer maintenance, leaving operating costs to non-tax revenues. But the great bulk of all historic sites in the country are privately owned and operated—by historical societies, patriotic organizations, private corporations, or in some instances by individuals. Here finance becomes a critical problem. Endowments are so few—and, where they exist, usually so small—that they can be disregarded. This leaves revenue from admissions, sales, and ingenious minor sources as the basic support of the privately-owned site or shrine.

The attractiveness of any site to the public is a mixture—in varying proportions—of three basic ingredients: the significance of the site or shrine, the presentation of the story it represents, and its location. To test some of the folklore and clichés about the location and financing of historic sites, a questionnaire was recently sent to fifty-seven carefully selected sites and shrines, including for comparative purposes a famed specialty museum (of historical nature) in the East, which is for historical reasons inauspiciously located; monument-museums in the old Northwest and the Southwest; a historically-oriented amusement park in the Plains; and a totally non-historical but educational tourist attraction on the Pacific coast. It included all the major restorations and reconstructions in the country, and a large assortment of historic buildings ranging from the House Where Lincoln Died (Washington, D. C.), and the Oldest House in St. Augustine (Florida) to the Mission San Francisco de Solano (Sonoma, California).

Of the fifty-seven sites queried, forty-four responded, thirty-four in sufficient detail to be useful for all aspects of this survey. One—a national monument in the author's state—refused to answer the questions on the possibly correct ground that the proposed study was of no value. Detailed financial data were submitted in confidence, hence the paucity of even guarded citations to sites.

Nineteen of the sites responding in complete detail are privately owned and operated, thirteen are state owned and operated, two are federal projects. Three (Mt. Vernon, Greenfield Village, and New Salem) have an annual attendance of over 1,000,000. Four range between 300,000 and 500,000. Three range between 100,000 and 200,000; one between 50,000 and 100,000. Attendance at the remaining thirteen is under 50,000 a year.

Significance

Why do people visit a site? Obviously they have heard or read something that piques their curiosity, convinces them that this is something they should see. This means that they will go in droves to the home of George Washington, Thomas Jefferson, or Abraham Lincoln, while they will go in lesser numbers to the home of Mark Twain, Daniel Webster, or George Washington Carver—and will not go at all to the home of John Doe unless it was designed by Frank Lloyd Wright. They will go in large numbers to a restoration or reconstruction that recaptures an important era or eras in our history—to a Sturbridge, a Greenfield Village, or a Virginia City. They will visit a Gettysburg in larger numbers than a Pea Ridge, a Ticonderoga before a Ligonier, an Astoria or a Bent's Fort before the lesser posts of the great West. Significance is a prime factor in the attractiveness of any site.

Location

Location is perhaps equally important. Mohammed may go to the mountain, but today he is much more likely to go if he can drive at least to its base and preferably to its summit—and park conveniently.

Clearly, the only sensible place to develop a historic shrine if you want to be readily accessible to the public (i.e., to draw huge throngs and educate as many people as possible, as well as derive large gate receipts and heavy revenues from sales) is at the intersection of two major interstate highways, on a high hill commanding the surrounding countryside, near a major population center or centers, convenient to airports and railroads, with a distinctive and unmistakable architecture which impresses itself as a trade mark on the public consciousness. Mt. Vernon has the site and the distinctive architecture, it is near a major urban area, and it has a major parkway built to its gate, but there are few passersby to attract. People plan ahead to go to Mt. Vernon. Williamsburg has the architecture, but no visibility from a distance. The

Castillo de San Marcos has the architecture, a heavy tourist population, nearby traffic arteries. The Mission San Xavier del Bac dominates the desert horizon for many miles out of Tuscon, but lacks the other prerequisites. Indeed only one shrine in the country meets every specification of ideal location: the Western Heritage Center at Oklahoma City, now in the process of construction. And few shrines can choose their location: they are already historically rooted to a specific site regardless of disadvantages.

The specific correlation of attendance to proximity to major highways—one factor in location—is like adding apples and oranges, and is even further complicated by the present state of traffic counts. These are computed differently from state to state. Some separate commuter traffic from tourist; others differentiate commercial vehicles from non-commercial; most are undiscriminating total counts. To the site in the midst of the city, city traffic count clearly is less meaningful than the through-traffic count that can be approximated for the rural site far enough removed from the city to eliminate commuter traffic. But in the latter instance one highway may be heavily travelled by commercial traffic (intercity or from a nearby gravel pit, for instance), another relatively free of such vehicles.

But traffic counts—particularly discriminate, rural traffic counts— do offer a combined indicator to two important factors in attendance: (1) the unintending visitor, the person who is just driving by and on the spur of the moment decides to stop, and (2) the through tourist who plans to visit a site or two,if he does not have to detour too far (and too long) from his predetermined path. Comparing traffic counts taken by the state highway department at a sufficient distance from the city to eliminate most if not all of the purely local traffic, and allowing two and one-half people per car, it seems clear that nearly everybody who visits Charlottesville, Virginia, visits Monticello;—but these are traffic figures for local highways and involve no major tourist routes. Mt. Vernon, with that parkway built from Washington to its gates, attracts one car in five in a traffic count which includes two major north-south routes in addition to the parkway. Cooperstown, N. Y., nine miles from a main artery (U.S. 20), though well established in the public consciousness, draws only the equivalent of one car in twenty of the traffic on Route 20 although it is also served by a second state highway, and by the New York Thruway which lies only a few miles north of U. S. 20. The computations involved in establishing statistically precise correlation between such diverse figures would defy a 7090 computer.

The only clearly meaningful figures uncovered in this survey were those from Wisconsin. Here carefully discriminate traffic counts on all routes near two sites—both of less significance and less public acceptance than the Mt. Vernons or the Alamos, and both lacking major poulation centers in the near vicinity—show clearly that one (the Villa Louis at Prairie du Chien, Victorian mansion of the fur-trading Dousman family) attracts 3.5% of the local highway traffic, while the second (the Wade House, midnineteenth century stagecoach tavern midway between Sheboygan and Fond du Lac) draws 4.5% from the state highway and the scenic drive which intersect at its site.

Any site counts on a substantial number of return visitations, often local residents bringing guests. It therefore seems a safe conclusion that if there were a large population center nearby and if finances provided a more adequate promotional budget, these Wisconsin figures could be raised substantially and that at least 5%, perhaps 7%, of traffic count could be a thoroughly reasonable possibility. If either Wisconsin site had the clear national stature of a Mt. Vernon, or the national appeal of a Western Heritage Center, this again could be substantially raised, say to 10% or more. The Circus World Museum in the former winter quarters of the Ringling Bros. Circus at Baraboo, Wisconsin, offers corroboration of the advantage of a large nearby population. Lying midway between two major tourist attractions fifteen miles apart, the Dells of the Wisconsin River and Devil's Lake, the museum, now in its fourth season, has annually attracted an attendance approximating 15% of the tourist population of the two resorts. Granted the special nature of this temporarily resident tourist population, 15% here again makes 10% of transient tourists elsewhere seem a tenable and rational possibility.

Admissions

Admissions revenue bears a similarly inexact relationship to the size of the admissions fee. Where a fee is charged, it ranges today from ten cents to $2.50. Probably Mt. Vernon could charge a substantially larger admission fee than it does today and take in somewhat more money. But if the increase were great, the number of visitors would be greatly cut, and the probable public uproar would deter others. Besides, the purpose of preserving a site clearly

is not to make money, but to be an educational facility, a preserver
of an aspect of historic and cultural heritage. There is no legitimate
reason for charging more than enough to meet expenses. But not
many sites make expenses today, and are consequently inhibited by
lack of the necessary finances from doing all the maintenance and
presentation work they should. But in establishing fees, they must
balance their needs against those of the touring family of five that
arrives at the gates and, finding the price of admission above what
the head of the family feels the site is worth (or he can afford),
turns away disgruntled. Greater revenue through greater volume at
a lower fee is devoutly to be desired for the benefit both of the
public and the site. The question is where to fix the fee to get the
necessary—not necessarily the maximum—revenue, and how to attract the maximum number of people.

As I have already suggested, people come to sites about which
they know something interesting and/or favorable. Does this mean
paid advertising? Not necessarily. Mt. Vernon does not need to
advertise at all. The plantation of the Father of the Country is
something most tourists visiting Washington feel they should see.
They know it is there and they go—over a million of them a year.
Yet one major Eastern restoration which is firmly established in
public consciousness feels that advertising, because of the general
pattern of its visitation, is necessary. The nature and extent of the
restoration and its general area are such that it is a terminal desti-
nation for many of its visitors for whom overnight and eating
facilities must be provided. The restoration, which operates various
accommodations facilities—income from which is used to further
its historic program—naturally encourages use of these facilities.
It is to this end that its advertising is devoted. Still another large
combination museum and reconstruction, also rather firmly established in public approval but lacking eating and housing responsibilities, spends exactly one percent as much money on advertising as
the first restoration. Moreover it spends its entire advertising budget
on highway signs largely on one main artery running within nine
miles of its site, relies chiefly on word of mouth advertising by
satisfied visitors and on feature articles in newspapers and in select
periodicals of somewhat limited circulation.

Advertising is clearly more essential for those sites and shrines
not yet so widely known to, and accepted by, the public. But these
are precisely the institutions whose budgets inhibit advertising on

any large scale. Here billboards and pamphlets, with some use of radio and TV spots, are standard fare. But here, too, there are pitfalls for the unwary. The local site can hope for considerable free coverage from local and area newspapers, radio, and even television stations until it pays for some advertising in these media. Then, if one gets paid, quite understandably everyone demands cash.

There are many highly economical ways of advertising the less affluent site. The local chamber of commerce is almost without exception glad to help publicize a local attraction: a place where the tourist—or the wives of the delegates at the local convention—would want to go. Local hotel or motel desks and travel agencies are usually glad to distribute local site circulars. The road maps of the major gasoline companies are excellent places to be listed. The guide books and trip tickets of major automobile clubs cost money, but are well worth consideration in a limited promotional budget. The companies making place mats for restaurants in a given area, or more commonly along a given highway, are usually glad to include the good historic sites along the way—some for a fee, some for free. No Wall Drug Store type of saturation marker program for any historic site is known, but directional signs or blazers along nearby highways are widely used. They are not expensive, though in rural areas, particularly east of the Mississippi, many farmers expect a small fee for permitting the erection of a sign on their property. In some states the state highway department will include markers to historic sites on its intersection directional signs —particularly if the site is state (or state historical society) operated. Few, if any, sites use match box covers, an inexpensive but thoroughly unselective way of getting the word abroad. Decals were once even more widely used than they are today. But the unsolicited sticking of an unremovable decal to the bumper or windshield of an unsuspecting owner's automobile produced such violent reactions in so many cases that this device is more cautiously used today. More common is the sale of decals to those who request them—a regular part of the souvenir sale program at many sites today. Those so purchased are likely to be used.

Proprietors of every good site or shrine agree that the very best promotion is the word of mouth advertising of the satisfied customer. And the only money that produces the satisfied customer is money paid to insure a good show, worth seeing a second time, worth sending your friends to see.

Sales

At no site are admissions alone sufficient to meet expenses. Even the most modest operations, where an elderly person on social security tends the plant, cannot rely on admissions alone to meet long-range maintenance and repair costs. And obviously, the service so rendered is not likely to attract repeat visitations or strong oral recommendations to friends. So the problem of how else money can be raised as a normal part of day to day operations is universal.

Sales, as a useful supplement to admission revenues, are a major answer. Still decried in some quarters as undignified and in poor taste, they are used by leading museums the country over—the Metropolitan, the Museum of Natural History, the National Gallery, the Gilcrease, the Walker, for instance—to good advantage without loss of prestige because these institutions are careful about the line they carry. To sell souvenirs, it is not necessary to go in for over-printed T-shirts, inscribed water-pistols, or beanies. Postcards and slides are now nearly universally available. Note paper, tiles, etchings of the site surely are in keeping. So too are pamphlets or books about the site or about the period or persons it represents. And every site can use appropriate trinkets—appropriate to the period, the area, the nationality groups involved. Some institutions collect and market period antiques, duplicated from or unneeded in their collections. In most institutions, every penny legitimately gained makes possible better maintenance, a better program, better service to the visitor, even expansion of the restoration, reconstruction, or plant.

Every dollar of admissions should yield a dollar of sales, goes a saw that for years has made the rounds of those engaged in site operation. If true, remarkably few sites have ever achieved the goal. In fact in this survey, including as it does so many major sites and restorations, it is remarkable that only three achieve this standard: one major reconstruction in the Northeast, and two historic houses —and you will not guess which—in Virginia. Two more come respectably close: a fort on the western fringes of the East, and a house on the eastern fringes of the Midwest. Only two others—another midwestern house and Thomas Jefferson's mansion—take in nearly two thirds as much from sales as from admissions.

More significant than matching sales and admissions dollars is the per capita expenditure of each visitor to the site. The picture here is even less reassuring. Only that same Northeastern reconstruction, and one of the two Virginia houses, averages over a dollar's worth to each visitor, though a Southwestern monument-museum comes close, as does the second Virginia house. At the other end of the line is the site in the so-called "postcard" class, where the average tourist expenditure falls between five and ten cents per capita. Here, surprisingly, one finds some of the most extensive and most heavily visited sites and shrines as well as most of the smaller and most impecunious operations. Clearly such revenue returns are unnecessarily low, especially where visitation is heavy. An imaginative example of what can reasonably be done is that of Old Economy, at Ambridge, Pa., a state-owned site where a private group of associates has in just a few years built up sales which grossed somewhat more than paid admissions and averaged nearly eighty-five cents per paid visitor. The national average, extrapolated from the sites queried in this survey, comes closer to forty cents expenditure per capita; the ratio of revenue from sales to revenue from admissions to 55.8%.

But here, too, the site administrator's path is thorny. Nothing repels most visitors more than what is loosely termed "over-commercialization". "Junk" cheapens the whole show, alienates many. Having only high-priced items repels the general public, gives an unwelcome impression that the site caters only to the wealthy, and certainly discourages the children who are often the freest spenders—at least for the less expensive items. And some seemingly appropriate and very attractive items just won't sell at a particular site. Clearly the line carried is important, as is the display, the sales service—in short the merchandising of the goods. The mark-up must be high on a necessarily limited number of sales to pay the indirect, as well as the direct, costs and still make a decent profit. And at its worst, pushing too hard for the tourist dollar leads to the development of a tourist trap so detrimental to the whole field that leaders are already calling for accreditation measures.

From a melange of confusing statistics, these conclusions can be drawn. A weighted mixture of significance, presentation, and location can draw attendance at an average historic site or shrine approximating between five and ten percent of the non-commuting traffic of the vicinity. A nationally notable site or shrine can draw far more. And, with a carefully selected line of appropriate, dignified souvenirs and literature, a site can readily earn between 50% and 100% of admissions revenue through sales.

Preservation of Historic Sites: Whose Responsibility?

Federal Responsibility

Edward M. Riley

Among those persons interested in historic preservation in the United States there is much confusion as to the spheres of activity that properly belong to private individuals or organizations and those that belong to the federal, state, or local governments. This paper cannot hope to resolve this confusion, but a brief discussion of the role played by the Federal Government in historic preservation may afford some clarification.

The preservation movement in the United States has developed in a unique way. Most European countries followed the lead of France in regarding historic remains as part of a national heritage to be inventoried, managed, restored, and protected by the national government. In the United States, this bureaucratic principle was not adopted; preservation of historic sites was in the beginning largely the work of individuals. Even today the source of the movement rests to a great extent in local initiative.

The Federal Government was brought, almost inadvertently, into the business of preservation. The veterans of the Civil War held reunions and encampments on the battlefields shortly after the war and conceived the idea that the battlefields should be preserved. These veterans became the leaders in Congress in the following decades, and developed widespread popular support of the idea, until in 1890 the Chickamauga-Chattanooga National Military Park was established. At the present time there are 28 areas relating to the Civil War in the National Park System.

There always has been a need for enlightened, well-directed local support for specific projects to obtain Federal participation. An outstanding example is the Independence National Historical Park in Philadelphia. It took the astuteness and tireless work of Judge Edwin O. Lewis, whose unselfish and patriotic motives were never questioned, to mobilize the local leadership in Philadelphia through the organization of the Independence Hall Association, and through that organization to win the support of the National Park Service, the Secretary of the Interior, the members of Congress, the Governor of Pennsylvania, and the city officials.

On the other hand, grass roots support and able local leadership will fail to secure Federal participation in a project if sympathetic leadership in Congress is lacking. The earliest type of general legislation to provide for the preservation of historical, archeological, and scientific sites and objects, the Antiquities Act of 1906, was the direct result of Congressional leadership. Archeologists and many other interested persons deplored the wholesale looting of the prehistoric cliff dwellings in the Southwest, and the clerk in the Public Lands Office was powerless to stop it. Congressman John F. Lacey of Iowa, who had no cliff dwellings in his district, became deeply interested in the problem. Fortunately, he had the vision to promote this piece of wise legislation and to broaden the act to cover various aspects of preservation. The act empowers the President to establish national monuments on Federal lands, and to protect historic and scientific landmarks. It provides a penalty for unauthorized excavations or destruction of any historic or prehistoric remains. The Antiquities Act has been used many times by different Presidents to protect historical, archeological, and scientific monuments.

Another vital factor affecting the Federal role in preservation is the degree of leadership in the executive department. Until 1916 there was no National Park Service. When established as a bureau of the Department of the Interior, it was given responsibility for the administration of national parks, monuments, and historic sites and directed to "conserve the scenery and the natural and historical objects and the wild life therein and to provide for the enjoyment of the same in such manner and by such means as will leave them unimpaired for the enjoyment of future generations."

When Stephen Mather was appointed the first director of the National Park Service, he found the historical properties acquired by the Federal Government scattered among three agencies, each with a different set of rules and regulations, and each bureau regarding the historical properties as secondary interests to its major purpose. Mr. Mather believed that there was need for an aggressive Federal program of historic preservation. He urged that all historical properties of the Federal Government be placed under one agency and that they be treated as a major, not a minor, asset. Mr. Mather did not live to see this consolidation take place, but his successor, Horace M. Albright, was able to achieve this goal. In 1933 all Federal properties acquired for historical purposes were placed in the custody of the National Park Service.

With this new responsibility, it was necessary to determine the type of historical program to be undertaken. To analyze this problem, an independent study was undertaken by J. Thomas Schneider, financed by a grant from John D. Rockefeller, Jr. Mr. Schneider, an eminent lawyer and special assistant to the Secretary of the Interior, made a careful survey of the historical programs of European countries and the United States. When the results of his study were published, they provided the basic data for new legislation. In 1935 the Historic Sites Act was enacted. This act enunciated for the first time a Federal policy toward the preservation of historic sites: "It is a National policy to preserve for public use historic sites, buildings, and objects of National significance for the inspiration and benefit of the people of the United States."

The Historic Sites Act of 1935 provided for a National Survey of Historic Sites and Buildings. To aid in the evaluation process, the act provided for an advisory board of eleven members eminent in the fields of history, archeology, architecture, and human geography.

In addition, a consulting committee of eight members was appointed to assist in the evaluation process. The act also provided for a broad basis of cooperative effort with states, communities, and individuals, but, according to the act, no financial commitments can be made without prior appropriation of funds by the Congress.

The following criteria are used by the consulting committee and the advisory board in evaluating historic sites and buildings:

1. Structures or sites at which events occurred that have made an outstanding contribution to, and are identified prominently with, or which best represent, the broad cultural, political, economic, military, or social history of the Nation, and from which the visitor

may grasp the larger patterns of our American heritage.

2. Structures or sites associated importantly with the lives of outstanding historic personages.

3. Structures or sites associated significantly with an important event which best represents some great idea or ideal of the American people.

4. Structures which embody the distinguishing characteristics of an architectural type specimen, exceptionally valuable for a study of a period style or method of construction; or a notable structure representing the work of a master builder, designer, or architect.

5. Archeological sites which have produced information of major scientific importance by revealing cultures, or by shedding light upon periods of occupation over large areas of the United States. Such sites are those which have produced, or which may reasonably be expected to produce, data affecting theories, concepts, and ideas to a major degree.

6. Every historic and archeological site and structure should have integrity—that is, there should not be doubt as to whether it is the original site or structure, and, in the case of a structure, that it represents original materials and workmanship. Intangible elements of feeling and association, although difficult to describe, may be factors in weighing the integrity of a site or structure.

7. Structures or sites of recent historical importance, relating to events or persons within 50 years, will not, as a rule, be eligible for consideration.

Twenty-eight years have passed since the Historic Sites Act became law. What role has the Federal Government through the National Park Service played in historic preservation?

Since 1935 the number of historical areas administered by the National Park Service has increased from 59 to 103. This increase has provided the Service with a better balanced historical program with sites related to all of the principal periods of American history.

During the years of the Depression the Park Service, through the Civilian Conservation Corps, gave direct assistance to many states in the development of historical properties. After the Second World War it assisted in the transfer of 41 pieces of Federal surplus property to the states for historical purposes.

Recognizing that many aspects of the movement for historic preservation lay outside the authority of a governmental bureau, the National Park Service assisted in 1949 in the establishment of the National Trust for Historic Preservation, a private organization that serves as a clearing house for all preservation activity in this country. The National Trust plays an increasingly important role in the field of preservation.

The Service encouraged the development of the Historic American Buildings Survey, begun in 1934 as a device to employ architects made idle by the economic depression. Allowed to lapse during the Second World War, the survey was resumed by the Service in 1957. It has accumulated a large body of detailed information concerning historic buildings through cooperative efforts with the American Institute of Architects, the Society of Architectural Historians, the National Trust for Historic Preservation, and the Library of Congress.

It has conducted the National Survey of Historic Sites and Buildings, authorized by the Historic Sites Act of 1935. A total of 27 studies are completed, ten studies are in progress, and all studies are scheduled for completion by 1966. To date, 404 sites and buildings have now been recognized as of national significance. One study, *Soldier and Brave,* concerning Indian and military affairs in the trans-Mississippi West, has been published, and another study is ready for publication.

In 1956 the Park Service established a Registry of National Historic Landmarks, as an outgrowth of the National Survey of Historic Sites and Buildings. To expedite the study of sites, the field of American history was divided into 22 periods or themes to cover all major periods of human history from the earliest known Indians to the emergence of the United States as a world power. Criteria were developed to evaluate the national significance of various sites and buildings. Identification of buildings with exceptional architectural values, and of archeological sites with major scientific interest, are included in the criteria.

The National Survey and the Registry are the first efforts of the Federal Government at systematized classification of historic sites. It is evident that classification of sites is essential to the development of any adequate program of historic preservation in the United States. The effectiveness of the movement to preserve significant historic sites and buildings will be heightened by the setting up of official state and local registers to supplement the work of the Federal Government. Some localities, for example, New Bern,

North Carolina, have carried out excellent programs of local classification, but classification must be nation-wide to be effective.

The problem has been greatly intensified by the population explosion and the new orientation in this country towards living in cities. The Urban Renewal Administration since the Housing Act of 1954 has become a most important factor in historic preservation. It should be noted, however, that urban renewal is a local program, bolstered by Federal financial assistance. It must be locally initiated, locally administered, and locally planned and carried out. Federal funds cannot be used to restore historic structures; actual restoration must be undertaken through some state or local public agency or private group. Urban renewal can be a powerful force in preservation. This was shown by the College Hill Demonstration Project in Providence, Rhode Island.

What then are the responsibilities of the Federal Government in the movement for historic preservation?

The Federal Government's (i.e., the Park Service's) responsibilities are limited by law to the preservation of sites and buildings of obvious national importance. Even in this restricted field, the Federal Government has relied largely on interested local groups to initiate preservation projects. No indications exist that this policy will be changed. This nation is too large, and its cultural patterns too diverse, to permit the Federal Government to assume a bureaucratic role in historic preservation like that taken by the national governments of Europe.

The field of historic preservation is a large one requiring the cooperative efforts of federal, state, local, and private agencies to assure the preservation of the nation's heritage. The need is for better cooperation. For example, the Park Service has high scholarly standards and a wealth of experience in the classification of historic sites. It is willing, within the availability of staff and funds, to share its experience in historic preservation with others. More use should be made of this source of knowledge by interested groups.

Social and physical change now taking place in the United States is accelerating the loss by demolition of important and irreplaceable structures. The Federal Government alone is not the proper defense against this destruction; it must be found in the combined efforts of all levels of government. These governments, however, can only reflect the wishes of the citizenry.

State Responsibility

Clement M. Silvestro

State governments have been assuming a greater and greater responsibility for the preservation of historic sites and buildings in the past 20 years. This is revealed clearly in the American Association for State and Local History's recently conducted survey of historical agencies in the United States. A similar pattern has developed at the federal and local levels of government, so that today, all levels of government share in the responsibility for preserving historic sites and buildings. What at one time was unusual has now become commonplace.

Up to World War II, the preservation of historic sites and buildings was primarily the responsibility of private groups. Private philanthropy remains strongly active in this field, but as interest in the historic preservation movement has broadened, so has the clamor for public support of these projects. Architectural historians, archaeologists, city planners, urban renewal specialists, architects and building contractors, art historians, conservationists, politicians, state park officials, and just plain do-gooders have joined the volunteer and professional members of historical associations in demanding support and action in this relatively new field. A large and articulate segment of our citizenry has concluded that historic preservation is a legitimate government responsibility which, like education and social welfare, needs public support and money because private resources alone are not adequate to do the job.

Is this development startling? Not necessarily. There is ample precedent for state action and participation in the field of historic preservation. After all, the conservation, interpretation, and presentation of historic sites and buildings is merely an extension of the state's acknowledged responsibility for the collection, preservation, and dissemination of its history. In America, this has become a well-established tradition.

The tradition has its roots in the expanding responsibilities of publicly-supported historical societies, historical commissions, and associations. Early historical societies were private organizations chartered by their state governments. Toward the middle of the nineteenth century almost every state had a historical society. In the Midwest the founding of state societies predated statehood, and in this same region developed the idea that it was the responsibility of the state to collect and preserve its historic records, and to educate future citizens in the history and accomplishments of the state. State societies requested and in many cases received public money for accomplishing these objectives, thereby establishing the precedent of state support for historical activities.

In the early decades of the twentieth century, the departments of archives and history and the historical commissions took their places next to the state-supported historical societies. This was particularly the case in those states where the state-wide historical society preferred to remain a private institution, and in those few instances where state governments had refused to give public support to private historical societies. Eventually, all the private historical societies that received large amounts of public funds were designated as official state agencies, even in those cases where they retained private control over their operations. Today there is not a state in the Union that does not have some official or semi-official agency that has the primary and recognized responsibility for the preservation and dissemination of the state's historic heritage. The tradition and precedent for state support of this historical heritage is now accepted fact. If you are skeptical about this conclusion, let me just point out that if all the legislation dealing with historical activity at the state level were brought together, it would comprise a volume of over 1000 pages. During this past summer, in an effort to build up our research and information collection, the American Association asked state historical agency directors for copies of all laws in their own state pertaining to historical societies, historic sites, historical commissions, archives and records management programs. Earlier studies did suggest that the amount of such legislation was great, but no estimates could have prepared us for the deluge of material that flowed into the Madison office.

Much of the legislation is similar. The states which were first to receive public support for their historical activities set the pattern. Yet, there are differences as well as similarities, both in the bulk and the quality of state legislation concerning historical activity. Not all states have comprehensive laws dealing with history activities, as do Minnesota, Pennsylvania, Wisconsin, or North Carolina, for example. As to quality, few can claim, as does the Pennsylvania Historical and Museum Commission, that the original act which created the Commission in 1913 was written in such broad and flexible terms that there is little need for change even today. The act grants, directly or indirectly, just about every power that the Commission could hope to exercise. Not all states are so blessed.

There is a vast difference in the administrative arrangement for governing and executing the various historic functions in each of the states. Our Association learned this from our survey of historical societies. In some states all historical activities are centralized under one strong state historical agency (the research library, archives, records management, historic sites and markers, publications, etc.). In other states these major functions are handled separately by smaller commissions or divisions attached to a larger state agency such as the Secretary of State's office, the Department of Administration, or the State Parks Commission. Local and regional traditions are also important.

But significantly, only a *small* amount of this legislation deals specifically with historic sites and buildings. The states early accepted the responsibility for developing historical libraries and archives commissions, but providing statutory arrangements for preserving historic buildings seems to be largely a development of the past 20 years. The concept of preserving sites and buildings as a responsibility of state government is relatively new. In a study presented at the Williamsburg conference on historic preservation, Charles Hosmer of Principia College, Illinois, pointed out that the movement to preserve buildings in the United States has been largely the work of private individuals and organizations. There is little evidence of direct state action in the historic house field in the nineteenth century. Of course there is the well-known case of the Has Brouck House in New York, purchased by the state in 1850. In 1856 the State of Tennessee paid $88,000 for the Hermitage, but it permitted the heirs of Andrew Jackson to occupy the house for nearly 50 years thereafter. In 1887 Robert T. Lincoln presented his family house in Springfield to the State of Illinois. The house was shortly thereafter opened to the public as a historic house museum under state control. In California the Native Sons of the Golden West bought Sutter's Fort in Sacramento and turned it over to the state in 1891. But other than these isolated instances, there was little state activity in the preservation of historic sites and buildings. Obviously this was an area beyond the immediate interest of historians and state historical society directors, who at the time were more anxious to secure legislative support for establishing departments of archives and history and historical commissions to preserve public records. The efforts of a Reuben Gold Thwaites in Wisconsin or a Floyd Shoemaker in Missouri to popularize history by marking historic sites were unique and not at all typical. For many years the preservation of historic sites and buildings was of peripheral interest to historians and historical agency directors alike.

In matters of developing historic sites and buildings, the states, it would seem, took their cue from the federal government and from private organizations. Because the federal government took the initiative in this field and provided a pattern for state governments to follow, we find many historic sites owned by states under the jurisdiction of state conservation departments or state park and recreation commissions. Three key federal statutes have had a large influence on the pattern of state action in the preservation of historic sites and buildings. These are the 1906 Antiquities Act, the 1916 National Conservation Act, which established the National Park Service, and the 1935 Historic Sites Act. The last act was the important one in making state governments and their state historical agencies recognize that the conservation and interpretation of sites and buildings was as important as the preservation of historical records, books, and manuscripts.

What is the current overall picture? Today the state agencies responsible for administering historic sites and buildings fall into two major categories. First are the publicly-supported historical societies, commissions, memorial boards, and departments of archives and history. Second are the state park deparments, a term used interchangeably with state agencies designated as state park and recreation boards, conservation departments, or land resources and public lands departments. The chief difference between the groups is that the first is history-oriented, while the second is conservation-oriented (land resources for fish, bird, and game preserves, reforestation, or park and recreational uses).

Administration of historic sites was put under the jurisdiction of state park departments for two major reasons. First, state governments simply adopted the federal procedure, and the federal government had put the administration of historic sites of national significance under the jurisdiction of the National Park Service. California and Florida are two good examples. Secondly, in the earlier years of the historic sites development, publicly-supported historical agencies did not consider the administration of sites a function of the historical society. Only when historical societies broadened their functions did these state historical agencies move into the field of historic sites administration.

The present dichotomy raises a perennial question: shouldn't the administration of historic sites and buildings be under the direct administration of the history-oriented agencies instead of the state parks? Historical agency directors sometimes feel that sites under the jurisdiction of state parks are often neglected because these departments are frequently headed by conservationists and naturalists whose interest in history is negligible. Specialists with training in history, so necessary for the proper development of sites, are seldom hired in these departments. Effective interpretation of the story being presented at these sites is often superficial or nonexistent.

Freeman Tilden, in his book *The State Parks: Their Meaning in American Life* (New York, 1959), has defended the administrative arrangement which puts historic sites under the control of state parks. He maintains that there are many problems common to both types of operation: for example, such matters as land acquisition, construction of facilities, protection, maintenance, interpretation, and public relations. He also points out that the arrangement permits employment of a wider range of technical personnel. It makes possible, Tilden says, the application of coordinated policies and practices designed to make available to the public the state's natural and cultural resources and thus provide a broader base of public support.

His forceful argument has merit, and on a theoretical level, it is even convincing. But disillusionment comes rapidly when one has had a chance to observe what the actual practices are. On the optimistic side, state park departments and state historical agencies have made great strides in working together, particularly where there is joint administration of historic sites. Yet the whole problem needs further study. Certainly valuable indications of what the best administrative arrangement is can only come from the results of an impartial inquiry into the present system. Historical agency directors must face the reality that the state park officials will not of their own accord turn over to them the historic sites under their jurisdiction, or vice versa. Nor must we overlook the fact that some state-supported historical agencies may not want to undertake the added responsibility. Further complicating the picture is the ample evidence that state park officials are becoming more and more interested in historic sites. The obvious conclusion is that the pluralistic arrangement for administering state-owned historic sites is a permanent one.

In slightly more than half of the states, the state park commission has jurisdiction over historic sites. Of these, the California Division of Beaches and Parks has a model program. It is based directly on that of the National Park Service. Two factors at work in California have made this organization unique. Of primary importance was the guiding hand of Newton Drury in the development of the program. Drury, who gave such long and distinguished service to the National Park system, was instrumental in establishing a strong history section within the Division of Beaches and Parks. The second major influence was the royalties that California enjoyed from offshore oil lands. The lavish funds from these royalties permitted the department to hire a staff of competently trained historians to develop their historic sites.

There are 22 state-supported historical agencies that have jurisdiction of historic sites. In at least seven of these states there is some joint jurisdiction between the state historical agency and the state park department. In still other instances, the historical agency director is an advisor on the historic memorial commission or state park board. Outstanding programs exist in New York, Pennsylvania, North Carolina, and Ohio. The state historical agencies in these states have ten or more sites under their jurisdiction. The Tennessee Historical Commission has indirect jurisdiction over 25 historic sites. Actually the sites are administered by local preservation groups who receive subsidies from the state through the commission.

As more and more publicly-supported historical societies came to recognize that the preservation of historic sites and buildings is an extension of the state's responsibility for preserving its heritage, more societies have taken control of historic sites in their states. In other instances, separate historical commissions have been organized and historic sites transferred to them. The Georgia Historical Commission was organized as recently as 1950 and now has 15 sites and a budget of over $100,000 a year, not including capital improvements. State legislatures have recently established historical commissions in Connecticut and Texas.

In at least two states, sites formerly under control of state park departments have been reassigned to state historical agencies. In the last session of the Kansas legislature, two historic properties formerly under the jurisdiction of the park commission were transferred to the Kansas State Historical Society. Recently the Pennsylvania legislature assigned two sites under the jurisdiction of the Pennsylvania Department of Water and Conservation to the Pennsylvania Historical Commission.

State-supported historical agencies should have an important role in the administration of historic sites, if not directly, certainly jointly with state park commissions, and at the very least, in an advisory capacity where direct or joint administration is not possible.

Other developments in recent years have accounted for the expanded responsibility of state governments in the areas of preserving historic sites and buildings. Such developments include historic district legislation and urban renewal activity. Agitation is increasing for state enabling legislation in the area of historic districting to protect historic areas and buildings. Historic preservation groups, architectural and art historians, architects, and others have faced the realization that their efforts to preserve historic sites and buildings can only succeed with the restrictive or enabling power of state governments to prevent the destruction of historic areas. Since all local government derives its power from the state, enabling legislation is necessary for local action, and consequently more and more pressure can be expected at the state level to enact this type of legislation. The states along the Eastern seaboard which have heretofore resisted all efforts to seek state support for preservation projects, seem now most eager to pass enabling acts establishing historic districts. Connecticut is the most recent state to pass historic district legislation, and the passage of the act came only after such a battle that the legislators almost didn't get to the state's *major* legislation for the session! Again there is a precedent here for the state to act, and it *must* act.

Legislation protecting historic areas can in some ways be an extension of the type of legislation that was passed in earlier years for protecting Indian mounds and archaeological sites. Also important at the state level is enabling legislation that will permit county boards to make appropriations to county historical societies. It interests us because today many local historical societies preserve historic houses and use these buildings as their museum headquarters.

Federal legislation permitting states to preserve historic sites and areas is important, and should be pointed out. As reported in the July 1963 issue of *History News*, the Minnesota legislature gave the Minnesota Historical Society a special $80,000 appropriation in a natural resources bill for the establishment and maintenance of historic sites. The appropriation came through the natural resources bill because in 1960 the Congress passed the Federal Open Spaces Act, which provides states with funds on a matching basis to buy open spaces surrounding urban communities for the development of conservation programs—to protect fishing streams, hunting lands, rural parks, picnic areas, and public beaches. Conservation of historic areas has been justly considered an important part of this program. This is the newest development that permits the state to act in the preservation of its historic heritage.

In all these developments the state historical agency should be a direct participant, and, in fact, assume the leadership for influencing this legislation. If the state historical agency does not wish to assume this role, it should at least be prepared to advise and guide the groups that do. If the present trend continues, we shall expect to see more, and not less, legislation at the state level relating to historic sites, buildings, and districts, as well as other enabling legislation to permit local groups to carry out their educational objectives.

Municipal Responsibility

Margaret B. Tinkcom

Had anyone twenty-five or thirty years ago raised the questions: "What role should the city play in the preservation of its historic buildings or of its architectural monuments?" "Has it any responsibility at all in this field?", the answer would have been, in all likelihood, "No. A city has no responsibility in this sphere." And a good many persons might have added, "No responsibility at all, thank goodness."

Preservation of historic buildings and areas has always been a private matter in the United States, fostered by interested persons,

and by historical societies and other local groups usually concerned
with the preservation of a single building of traditional interest to
the community. This is, of course, quite contrary to the European
practice. There, nearly every country, England, France, Sweden,
Denmark, the Netherlands, to name a few, has some sort of "Monuments Protection Act" currently in force. Stephen Jacobs relates this
difference in approach to the problems of historical preservation as
practiced in the United States and in Europe to the democratic
process as it developed here. He believes that a country which relied
on a tradition of decentralized authority would naturally make
preservation a matter of response to local demand, rather than leave
it in the hands of a central, and by analogy, an "aristocratic" authority.

Why did privately organized local groups instead of the municipal
governments take over the job of protecting our historical monuments? Many reasons have been given for this, among them, a
universal distrust of the integrity of the city fathers; fear of legal
red tape; and the notorious slowness to act which is characteristic
of all public bodies. Some unfortunate experiences with city governments—particularly in nineteenth-century New England, and the
tendency to imitate a successful example, notably that of the Mt.
Vernon Ladies Association which in the 1850's raised the required
$200,000 to purchase Washington's home, have also had a consider-
able effect on the development of the preservation movement in
the United States. The result was that preservation in this country
has remained essentially a private matter. In 1962 Charles B. Hosmer found that "about 70% of the preservation work was being
done by private individuals or non-governmental organizations; . . .
[and that] in 1962 nearly 68% of the preservations are in private
hands."

Notwithstanding this statistical evidence, a considerable change
has taken place in the climate of opinion among preservationists regarding the role city governments should play in the protection of
the visual evidence of a town's history, growth, and development.
It is now generally realized that "progress," in the guise of an
expressway, a new high-rise apartment, a shopping center or
super-market, can be difficult to arrest single-handed. And it has
become apparent that, if one or more governmental agencies, with
the authority of the whole city behind them, can be enlisted in
support of the threatened monument, there is a good chance, cer-

tainly a much better chance, that the disaster may be staved off.

Today, all across the United States, cities are taking an active part in the movement to preserve their historical records of brick and stone. They do this in various ways. One of the most common is to make use of an existing official agency, a department of parks, for example. As a matter of fact, in Philadelphia, the Fairmount Park Commission has been preserving a group of elegant eighteenth-century mansions for about one hundred years. Fairmount Park, as you may know, came into being in the 1850's in order to preserve the purity of the city's water supply. The preservation of the houses was incidental, but it has turned out to be a most fortunate incident for the city. Municipalities may also set up historic districts, where special regulations are applied to preserve the special character of the area. Usually such a district is under the jurisdiction of a review board. (In Williamsburg, Virginia, the city administrator is in charge; in Charleston, South Carolina, a board of zoning appeals has control.) In other cities, art commissions (as in Hartford, Connecticut), orginally appointed to consider the design of important, new public buildings, are encouraged to extend their interest to the preservation field.

Of all these possibilities the "historic district", and the "architectural control" imposed on such a district, offer the best opportunity for the preservationist. Charleston (in 1931) and New Orleans (in 1937) were the first cities to establish historic districts. Twenty years later the idea caught on in New England. Following the lead given by Beacon Hill in Boston (in 1955), a number of towns in Massachusetts (Salem in 1955 and Lexington in 1956); in Connecticut (Litchfield in 1959); and in Rhode Island have created historic districts.

In towns where the monuments are scattered, however, a historic district will not do the whole job. This is true of Philadelphia. Here, several areas, among them Society Hill (named for the Free Society of Traders, who owned much of this section, and not for the local aristocracy, as one might think); Southwark, the area, south of Penn's city proper, clustering around Gloria Dei Church; and Germantown, are full of eighteenth-century buildings well worth preserving. In other parts of town, there are significant, but isolated, buildings, John Bartram's house in Kingsessing, and Strickland's Naval Asylum, for instance. Faced with this situation, the Philadelphia preservationists proposed the creation of an advisory commission on public buildings which would have authority to act anywhere within the city, and in 1955 the Philadelphia Historical Commission was created by city ordinance, directed to survey the City of Philadelphia, list all the buildings in it worth preserving, and, insofar as is practicable, see that none of these is demolished or unsuitably altered. Clearly, cities today are assuming responsibility in the matter of preservation.

I should like to suggest that this is a divided responsibility—divided about equally between the city, defined as government, and the city, taken as the body of its citizens. In essence, it is the duty of the governing body to create a favorable climate in which historical monuments can continue to live; and at the same time is the duty of the citizens to make the fullest possible use of the opportunity the city government is offering them.

At the outset, the private citizens will have to take the initiative. And it may take a good strong push, from a local historical society, or chapter of the American Institute of Architects, joining together with other interested groups, to set the city's official machinery in motion. The first step involving a city government in the preservation business usually comes with the passage of an enabling ordinance permitting the appointment of an historic building commission or board of architectural review.

Showing a city council that it is a desirable thing to save historic buildings may not be too difficult. Everyone is for saving historic monuments just as everyone is against sin. However, persuading them that this is *legally* feasible may not be easy. Fortunately, the United States Supreme Court decision, Berman *v.* Parker [(1954) 348 US 26], has effectively disposed of any possibility that historical and architectural control violates any provision of the United States Constitution. It reads in part: "The concept of the public welfare is broad and inclusive. The values it represents are spiritual as well as physical, aesthetic as well as monetary. It is within the power of the legislature to determine that the community shall be beautiful as well as healthy, spacious as well as clean, well-balanced as well as carefully patrolled." This decision and the recent experience of other cities, all over the United States, give preservationists a strong argument, since government officials anywhere are more likely to consider a proposed program favorably if it can be shown that it has been tried successfully before.

In many cities the experience of the past half-dozen years has proved conclusively that a neighborhood characterized by a group of carefully restored houses is enormously profitable. The values of such buildings on the real estate market are considerably augmented and, with their increased sale value, their tax value has likewise gone up. This last, of course, brings money directly into the city coffers, and a proposal guaranteed to put money in the treasury always rings pleasantly in the ears of any public body.

The citizens' committee, having persuaded its local government to act, has a right to expect that the ensuing enabling ordinance will provide for the appointment of a knowledgeable board and endow it with sufficient power to become an effective agent on the preservation battlefield. For example, the Philadelphia Historical Commission operates under an ordinance which directs the Mayor to "appoint a commission consisting of the Director of Finance, the Commissioner of Public Property, and five persons *learned* in the traditions of the City and *interested in the preservation of the historic buildings of the City.*" This brief sentence makes two important statements. It provides for the inclusion on the board of two city officials, thus effecting an important liaison between the board and the city government. It also provides that the other members, the private citizen members, should be *learned* and *interested.* Both adjectives are important. (The Philadelphia Historical Commission includes historians and architects on its board, for example. A lawyer dedicated to the preservation of his city's historical buildings would also be a most useful member of any preservation commission.)

Since the Philadelphia Commission was the first such agency to be given jurisdiction over a whole city, it has served as a prototype for this kind of activity. It might be worthwhile, therefore, to review its operations briefly.

The Commission has two major duties directly stated in the ordinance and two equally important ones that are implicit but not stated. The first two are as follows:

1) To list all Philadelphia's buildings that are, in the opinion of the Philadelphia Historical Commission, worth preserving.
2) To prevent, if possible, the demolition or unsuitable alteration of any building on this list. (The Commission has the power to stay for six months any proposed alteration—or demolition —of which it does not approve. During that time the Com-

mission endeavors to persuade the owner to change his plans
for the building, and, failing that, to interest some other person or group of persons in taking it over.)

The Commission's two implied powers, or duties, are, first, the
right to review *all* plans for *any* sort of alteration to a certified
building. This is, of course, a corollary of the provision that the
Commission may prevent unsuitable alteration to such a building,
since in order to determine whether the proposed change is or is
not suitable, it is necessary to review carefully the plans for the
alteration. The second, which is a duty rather than a right, requires
the Commission to be informed of the "total" history of the area.
The Commission must know something of its economic background,
its social and cultural orientation, and its importance to the City.
This is necessary if it is to relate any given building or group of
buildings to the metropolitan complex and substantiate their importance in a way that will effectively demonstrate their right to
preservation.

Once a board of architectural review or a commission on historic
buildings has been created, the public has a right to expect that it
will do certain things:

   (1) All owners of buildings designated as historic and deemed
       worthy of preservation should be notified of this fact prompt-
       ly.
   (2) The commission should make public a clear statement of
       the criteria employed in designating buildings as historic.
   (3) They should also publish an outline of the procedures which
       owners must follow when presenting plans for the restora-
       tion or alteration of any certified building.
   (4) Furthermore, the board of review should be prepared to give
       specific and accurate advice on architectural matters to all
       owners planning to restore their houses. This will require
       the collection of as much information as possible about each
       certified building. A brief or title, to date the building, an
       insurance survey, to describe it, old photos and prints to
       reinforce and supplement the insurance record, are the basic
       needs.
   (5) Should an owner propose to demolish a historical building
       or alter it in a way that the commission believes to be un-
       suitable, he should, as a matter of course, be given an oppor-

tunity to appear before the board of review to explain his intention.

Since urban renewal is a fact of life in almost all of our major cities, a city government must pave the way for effective cooperation between its planning agency, the redevelopment authority, and the historic buildings commission. Plans should never be made for the renewal of any area where there are historical values to be preserved, until the district has been the object of intensive historical and architectural research. This, in Philadelphia, is the business of the Historical Commission, and, in general, I think it should be the task of the preservation agency. It will be the job of the city planners to juggle the recommendations of the preservation agency, the needs of institutions, the expressway locations, and the economics of rehabilitation, and come up with a reasonable solution based on more than short-sighted demands for "progress".

If the preservation agency has been consulted *while* plans for the area are being *drawn up, not* after they are in a final or semi-final state; and *if* a real effort is made to accommodate the differences between historical values and twentieth-century needs, urban renewal and historical preservation can get along together. If this is not done, the danger to the city is very real. And what a pity it would be if the future of our old cities should be sacrificed to the short-lived, and sometimes imaginary, requirements of the present!

There is, it seems to me, still one more area in which a city must exercise its authority if it is to meet its responsibilities in matters of preservation. This is in the housekeeping department: ordinances on zoning and uses, on building requirements, on property repair and occupancy, must be well drawn and well enforced, if restored buildings are to be given a climate in which they can survive. Overcrowding, for example, is one of the chief causes of slums. Demolition by neglect is another.

The design of new buildings which will stand in close juxtaposition to historic areas also should be a matter of concern to the city. Too great a contrast in design, too great a change in scale or material, should be avoided. Lack of planning in this respect can produce most unfortunate results.

Finally, I should like to return to that other segment of a city—the non-public segment, the citizens, the men and women of good will. I should like to make it clear that their responsibility does not end with the passage of the bill creating the historic district or setting up the historical commission to administer the city's monuments. This is, in fact, only the beginning. Everyone interested in preservation must remain on the job continually. For, like housekeeping, historical monument keeping is a never-ending task.

Local Historical Society Responsibility

W. Howard Adams

In 1962 President John F. Kennedy named a special consultant on the arts to study the nation's cultural situation with particular emphasis on the relationship of the federal government to the arts.

A few weeks ago, Mr. August Heckscher made his report to the President and as an important document on the intricate relationships between private and public agencies in a complex area not unrelated to the problems of historic preservation, it suggests some approaches at the local level that might be applied to matters before us today.

Mr. Heckscher called for no revolutions, issued no manifestos; rather, he simply reminded us that the present machinery of government is already grinding out, for better or for worse, what adds up to our national culture. It commissions works of art of all kinds, builds public buildings, strikes medals, designs stamps, unleashes urban renewal projects capable of altering a city landscape affecting millions, and, except for those few golden years of the early Republic, it has rarely done a good job.

Mr. Heckscher recommends instead of vast new governmental machinery or wholesale destruction of the old, some judicious repair and oil on what we already have.

Taking the same approach to solving some of the immediate problems of historic preservation on a local level, one needs to take a close look at the machinery already available and divine ways of putting it to work in the cause of preservation.

The problems of historic preservation are certainly greater than the simple efforts of finding an historic building and then raising the money to preserve it. Public and private agencies need to work together to achieve an imaginative, overall approach toward historic preservation in their community. This is no time to bicker over who does what. The more or less blind forces running against the community's efforts are formidable and will not be stopped by last-ditch fights over single buildings, after the bulldozers have moved in.

First of all, there are the usual ordinance-making bodies at every level of local government where the proper attention may pay dividends in protection and preservation of large areas. This may be a good place to begin with overt action, particularly where the historic district needs the legal protection of zoning controls.

Secondly, local urban renewal and area planning councils need and should expect expert guidance and assistance in determining what is and what is not worthy of preservation. Too often, we are prone to jump on these agencies for stupid and ill-advised programs without bothering first to give them a comprehensive picture of the importance of retaining some of the historic fabric of the past in the urban plans for tomorrow. In this conjunction, bankers deserve our special attention. Often their lack of vision encourages them to go the easy route of loans for new construction but nothing for rehabilitation, particularly if the property is located in a general area they consider a poor investment.

Thirdly, most local governments, including cities and counties, are spending each year more and more tax money in the loosely defined area called recreation. As our populaion changes in its tastes and interests, the concept of recreation will have to change too. Last year, the Stanford Research Institute made a revealing study of the recreational habits of Americans today.

On the basis of the Stanford study, it is estimated that possibly 50 million Americans actively participate in amateur art activities. You will have to take the word of this respectable institute that there are more people who play the piano than hold fishing licenses —there are more painters than hunters—twice as many people attended concerts and recitals as attended all our major league baseball games last year—more people went to the theater than the combined number that went boating, skiing, golfing, or skin diving —and to finish off these extraordinary statistics, only the Empire State Building attracts more visiting servicemen on leave in New York than the Museum of Modern Art. Statistics in the general area of museums and historic buildings follow the same pattern. Recently, it has been estimated that twice as many people visited museums and historic sites than attended all major sports events last year.

In Jackson County, Missouri, our own Park Department has already moved to shift some of its emphasis and is taking steps to incorporate educational projects into the usual recreational park activities of picnicking, hiking, boating, and so forth. The department has just completed a fifteen-year project of reconstructing the famous Fort Osage located by William Clark on the Missouri River in 1807. Governor Clark's site for the Fort makes an ideal spot for family outings in the twentieth century just as it provided military protection for families in the nineteenth century.

Recently, a large lake with the usual water recreation facilities was developed by the county. Now, in a remote corner of this vast wooded park, an outdoor museum of houses and buildings of the pre-Civil War period is being assembled into a village. Actual buildings, too modest and too remote to be restored on their original sites, are being carefully moved into this new museum area.

Just a few weeks ago, the park director commissioned a study of a possible location of a boat marina on the Missouri River. The site that is under consideration is one which includes a now dilapidated river-boat tavern built for the grand days of steam boating in the 1850's. The idea is to restore this relic of the region's history and use it as a part of a modern day recreational boating facility but with its historic fabric intact and presented in terms that should not offend the purists. After all, its original purpose was river travel, a pleasure that the twentieth century is beginning to rediscover in many parts of the country.

Now, who is to be the spark-plug in all of this? Why the historical society, of course, for no other group at the local level can muster *all* of the elements in the community into an effective agency for action. Who knows better the history of a place and at the same time the local politician, the public official, the banker—as well as the candlestick-maker? The practical solution of everyday problems is one of the great assets of this country and we should not be afraid to turn this American technique to the serious problems of advancing the cause of historic preservation.

Success will, of course, presuppose that the historical society has shed most of its nineteenth-century attitudes and does, in fact, truly represent the broadest possible cross-section of the local community, which is concerned with the difficulties of giving some sense of continuity in today's world of change regardless of race, creed, color, or pedigree. In other words, I am suggesting that we, at the local level, give new thought to what might be called the practical politics of historic preservation!

Contributors

Jonathan Daniels, Editor, *News & Observer*, Raleigh, North Carolina

Frederick L. Rath, Jr., Vice Director, New York State Historical Association, Cooperstown, New York

Wilcomb E. Washburn, Curator, Division of Political History, Smithsonian Institution, Washington, D. C.

Harold L. Peterson, Staff Historian, National Park Service, Washington, D. C.

Robert B. Inverarity, Director, Adirondack Museum, Blue Mountain Lake, New York

Merrill J. Mattes, Regional Chief, Division of History and Archaeology, National Park Service, Midwest Region, Omaha, Nebraska

James T. Forrest, Director, Museum of New Mexico, Sante Fe, New Mexico

John W. Jenkins, Chief, Western Museum Laboratory, National Park Service, San Francisco, California

Clifford L. Lord, Dean, School of General Studies, Columbia University, New York, New York

Edward M. Riley, Director of Research, Colonial Williamsburg, Williamsburg, Virginia

Clement M. Silvestro, Director, American Association for State and Local History, Madison, Wisconsin

Margaret B. Tinkcom, Historian, Philadelphia Historical Commission, Philadelphia, Pennsylvania

W. Howard Adams, President, Adams Dairies, Blue Springs, Missouri

Membership

Membership in the American Association for State and Local History is open to anyone interested in fostering the study, preservation and dissemination of localized history in the United States and Canada. Established in 1940, the Association is a non-profit, educational organization of state and local historical agencies in the United States and Canada. Individuals and institutions are eligible for membership.

Members of the Association receive copies of *History News,* a monthly publication featuring current activities of state and local historical societies, and copies of the *Bulletins,* as published. Complete publication lists are available from the Association's office; members receive a discount on publication orders. Members may attend the annual meetings of the Association and participate in its discussion and business sessions. Membership in the Association is $3.00 annually.

The Association founded and for five years published *American Heritage,* an illustrated magazine of American history. Management of the magazine has since been transferred to a professional publisher, with whom the Association shares control. Subscriptions to *American Heritage* may be sent to its offices at 551 Fifth Avenue, New York 17, New York.

Please address all inquiries regarding the Association to:

> *The American Association for State and Local History*
> *132 Ninth Avenue, N.*
> *Nashville, Tennessee 37203*

PUBLICATIONS OF
THE AMERICAN ASSOCIATION
FOR STATE AND LOCAL HISTORY

BULLETINS

A Guide to the Care and Administration of Manuscripts, by Lucile M. Kane.
The Management of Small History Museums, by Carl E. Guthe.
Local History Contributions and Techniques, by Benjamin W. Larabee, Edward M. Riley, and Bayrd Still.
Organizing a Local Historical Society, by Clement M. Silvestro.
The Local History Magazine and Its Publication, by Milton Hamilton.
Archaeology and Local History, by J. C. Harrington.
The Junior Historian Movement in the Public Schools, by H. Bailey Carroll.
A Publicity Program for the Local Historical Society, by J. Martin Stroup.
Using Volunteers in the Local Historical Society's Program, by Loring McMillen.
The Production of Local History Plays and Pageants, by Samuel Selden.
Broadcasting History: The Story Behind the Headlines, by Evelyn Plummer Read.
Church Archives and History, by Thomas H. Spence, Jr., Virgil V. Peterson, and Thomas F. O'Connor.

OCCASIONAL PUBLICATIONS

1963 Directory of Historical Societies and Agencies in the United States and Canada.	$2.00
The Present World of History, edited by James H. Rodabaugh.	$3.00
Ideas in Conflict, edited by Clifford L. Lord.	$3.00
The Cost of Freedom, by Frederick L. Rath.	$1.00
New Horizons, by Clifford L. Lord.	$1.00

TECHNICAL LEAFLETS

Technical leaflets are published for the purpose of bringing useful information to persons working in the state and local history movement. The leaflets are published as inserts to *History News* and are available at $.10 each.

Order from:

The American Association for State and Local History
132 Ninth Avenue, N.
Nashville, Tennessee 37203